HOLIDAYS WITH
THE BILLIONAIRE BOYS CLUB

CARA MILLER

Want my unreleased 5000-word story
Introducing the Billionaire Boys Club
and other free gifts from time to time?

Then join my mailing list at

http://www.caramillerbooks.com/inner-circle/

Subscribe now and read it now!

You can also follow me on Twitter and Facebook

An Invitation from the Billionaire Boys Club

———

Midnight with the Billionaire Boys Club

———

Dreaming with the Billionaire Boys Club

———

A Promise from the Billionaire Boys Club

———

Engaged to the Billionaire Boys Club

———

A Surprise from the Billionaire Boys Club

———

Romance with the Billionaire Boys Club

———

A Billionaire Boys Club Wedding

———

Honeymoon with the Billionaire Boys Club

———

Billionaire Boys Club Babies

———

Italy with the Billionaire Boys Club

———

Life with the Billionaire Boys Club

———

A Billionaire Boys Club Autumn

———

Holidays with the Billionaire Boys Club

Kelsey tossed off the the covers and leapt out of bed. Her heart pounding, she ran to the bedroom door, pulled it open, and dashed into the hall.

As she breathlessly ran down the stairs, her mind raced through possibilities. There was no way that Tyler could have cooked Thanksgiving dinner, no matter how early he had got out of bed. Tyler was skilled at many things, but he wasn't an expert in the kitchen. Sadness welled up inside of Kelsey as she realized that she would need to admit her failure to make dinner for her family and guests — and accept that they would have to go to a restaurant today.

Kelsey reached the bottom of the stairs and glanced around. She and Tyler had explored this house during their honeymoon, but at the time they had been more focused on exploring each other than the house, so Kelsey wasn't sure where the kitchen was. But suddenly, she heard laughter, and she dashed toward the sound.

She ran through a doorway, and stopped abruptly at the sight before her.

Then she burst into tears.

As she stood in the entrance of the kitchen, Kelsey surveyed the scene that had made her so emotional. Steve was sitting at the breakfast table, eating a pastry and looking at his phone. Margaret stood next to Tyler. They had clearly been chatting.

And all over the kitchen, almost everywhere Kelsey looked, there were containers of food. Covered warming trays, glass containers full of cranberry sauce and green beans — every large surface in the kitchen was covered with dishes that Kelsey knew had been lovingly and expertly prepared by Margaret.

Prepared by Margaret for Kelsey. So she wouldn't have to race to put a Thanksgiving meal on the table.

"Oh, dear, did we wake you?" Margaret asked with concern as Tyler walked over to Kelsey and put his strong arms around her. Kelsey sobbed into his chest and Tyler kissed her hair.

"I'm OK," Kelsey finally sniffed. She looked up into Tyler's eyes.

"Do you want to get dressed?" Tyler asked her. "Then you can see what Margaret brought for us."

Kelsey nodded. "OK," she said, grateful for the suggestion. "Excuse me." And she left the room.

She slowly walked the same path she had run moments before. Her tears continued to fall. But instead of the tears of sorrow she had experienced when she had run down the stairs, Kelsey knew that these were tears of relief, gratitude, and love.

Fifteen minutes later, Kelsey re-entered the kitchen. Things had been shifted around, and Steve was no longer in the room. Tyler gave Kelsey a bright smile as she walked in.

"Are you feeling better?" Margaret asked.

"Yes, thank you," Kelsey said. She had taken a quick shower, and her damp hair was in a ponytail high on her head.

"Tyler said that you didn't get much sleep last night," Margaret commented, removing a cover from a glass bowl.

"We didn't," Kelsey said. "Thank you for cooking for us."

"It's my pleasure, Kelsey," Margaret said. "Tyler said weeks ago that you wouldn't have time to cook, but that it was your turn to make Thanksgiving dinner."

Kelsey glanced at Tyler, who winked at her.

Weeks ago, Kelsey thought, sighing to herself.

"He was right," Kelsey admitted. "I appreciate your help. Can I do anything?"

"Everything is pretty much set," Margaret replied. "The turkey should stay warm in the oven, and we've set up the buffet in the dining room. You'll just need to take the turkey, deviled eggs, and sauces out right before dinner. Oh, and pull the desserts out a few minutes before serving them, so they get to room temperature."

Kelsey walked over to the refrigerator and looked inside. Every shelf had Margaret's handiwork on it. Kelsey saw two pies, a glass container with luscious-looking cookie bars, and several other items before she closed the door.

"You outdid yourself, Margaret," Kelsey said sincerely. "Thank you."

Margaret beamed. "You don't have to keep thanking me," she said, "I know how hard you work. Anyway, it was quite fun. I've never made a Southern-style Thanksgiving before, but Ryan and I learned a lot while we were cooking."

"Will you and Steve join us? We'd love to have you," Kelsey said.

"Thank you, but no. We'll eat with Lisa and Ryan's family after we make our next stop."

"Stop?" Kelsey asked curiously.

"Margaret and Steve will drop Thanksgiving dinner off at the Hill house," Tyler said.

"Morgan's?" Kelsey asked in surprise.

"I'm amazed that you and Tyler had time to pick up extra groceries for them last night." Margaret said. "That was kind of you."

Kelsey realized that Tyler had given their Safeway purchases away. Saying that the food was for the Hill family was probably Tyler's way of explaining to Margaret why all of the food was in the house. She realized that that was probably where Steve was, putting the extra bags of food into the car.

Margaret continued, "Speaking of, we should get moving, otherwise Lisa will make everyone wait for us."

"Everyone?" Tyler said.

Margaret gave him a look. "It seems that Bill Simon has joined Bob on his annual Thanksgiving trip to play golf in Arizona, so that's one less person. You wouldn't know anything about that, would you?"

"No."

"In fact, I haven't seen much of Bill Simon lately," Margaret said, looking suspiciously at Tyler.

"Wasn't me," Tyler replied. "Tactec has been keeping me too busy to meddle. Bill's been working a lot lately. So maybe there's nothing wrong?"

"It's a little odd," Margaret said. "Are you sure that you aren't involved?"

"I could be, if that's what you want," Tyler teased.

"I don't. Stay out of it," Margaret warned.

"Maybe they broke up?" Tyler said brightly.

Margaret was thoughtful for a moment. Kelsey thought she was considering that possibility. Finally Margaret shook her head.

"Lisa would have said something," Margaret concluded. "At the very least she'd be moping around."

"Lisa Olsen mopes?" Kelsey asked in surprise.

Margaret and Tyler looked at her.

"When she's not getting her own way, yes," Tyler replied.

"It doesn't make any sense. Why haven't we seen him lately?" Margaret commented as Steve walked through the side door of the kitchen.

"Are you grilling Tyler about Bill Simon?" Steve asked in amusement.

"I don't know anything," Tyler said.

"It's better that way," Steve said. "Stay out of the emotional lives of your employers," he told Margaret. "That's my motto."

"You're about to drop Thanksgiving dinner off at Bob's ex-girlfriend's house," Tyler pointed out.

Steve shrugged. "Bob said to do it, so it's done. I'm not asking any questions about why."

"You know why," Margaret commented. "Bob's still in love with her."

"That's between them. All I have to do is drive the car and drop off an envelope."

"An envelope?" Tyler asked curiously.

"It's a check. Two of the girls are going to school now, and you know how Bob feels about that," Steve explained.

"I do," Tyler replied.

"That's nice of him," Kelsey said. She hadn't realized that Bob was helping Morgan's sisters pay for college, but she wasn't surprised after his comments in Chicago. Bob felt very strongly about education as a way to get out of poverty.

"See, we don't have to debate Bob's motives or emotional state. We just have to do the work," Steve commented.

"You aren't curious?" Margaret asked him.

"No," Steve replied.

"Well, I am," Margaret said. "It's fine, we can fight about this in the car on the drive back. Let's get going."

"Thank you very much for driving over," Kelsey said sincerely.

"It's fine. I had to come anyway," Steve commented.

"For the check?" Tyler asked.

"Bob always sends food to the Hill family over for the major holidays," Margaret commented, picking up her expensive purse.

"I didn't know that," Tyler said, glancing at Kelsey. She shook her head. She hadn't known that either.

"Everyone needs to calm down," Steve commented. "Bob and Lisa's lives are no different than they were a year ago. Bob's in denial, and Lisa keeps dating men who can't handle her success."

"And you say that you aren't paying attention," Tyler said.

"No, I said that I don't need to make it my business. It's my job to know what's going on," Steve replied.

"That's a fine line," Margaret said.

"One I don't need to cross. Are you ready?" Steve replied.

"Yes," Margaret said grumpily.

"I'm going to buy you a book. Find you a hobby," Steve teased.

"I have one. It's figuring out who's the next person who's moving into the estate," Margaret said.

"I'm guessing that you don't think it's Ryan and Jessica's next baby," Tyler commented.

"No, I do not," Margaret replied.

"That's troubling," Tyler commented.

"I don't know. If Bill doesn't show back up soon, you might be off the hook for now," Steve replied.

"Stop pretending you don't care!" Margaret shouted at Steve, who laughed at her reaction.

"Yes, Miss Nilsen," he said. "Let's go. Goodbye, you two."

"Goodbye, thank you," Kelsey said.

"Have a lovely Thanksgiving," Margaret said.

"You too. Bye," Tyler said, and Margaret and Steve left.

Tyler put his arms around Kelsey's waist. "Hi," he said, nuzzling her.

"You're trouble, you know that, right?" she said, looking up into his sparkling brown eyes. He leaned down and kissed her. "Thank you," Kelsey said.

"You're welcome," Tyler replied.

"So I guess we're all ready?"

"I think so. Do you want to see the dining room?" Tyler asked her.

"Sure," Kelsey said. Tyler released her and took her hand. They walked into the dining room, and Kelsey looked around in surprise.

When Margaret had said that they had set up the buffet, Kelsey was expecting large chafing dishes and fancy decorations, like at a hotel. But instead, it looked simple, just like something that Kelsey and her mom would have set up.

Fresh flowers in vases, a few autumn leaves scattered on the table, and pretty fall dinnerware. In fact, the food on the buffet was in family-size warming dishes exactly like the ones that Kelly North brought out during large gatherings.

Kelsey looked around, a little wistfully. If only she had had more time.

"What do you think?"

"It's beautiful. I couldn't have done a better job," Kelsey replied as Tyler put his arms around her once more and she leaned her back against him. She surveyed the room, then turned to face him.

"What if I had managed to make dinner?" Kelsey asked

Tyler looked at her, amusement in his brown eyes.

"Humor me. What would have happened to the food?" Kelsey pressed.

"I would have told Margaret that you had decided to cook. It wouldn't have been a big deal," Tyler said.

"I guess not," Kelsey said. "I guess they would have taken it to the Hill family."

"How do you feel about that?"

"About what?"

"About Bob still being involved with Morgan's family?"

Kelsey shrugged. "He's still involved with Morgan, so I'm not surprised."

"I didn't ask if you were surprised, I asked how you felt about it," Tyler said.

Kelsey sighed. "I need to be more like Steve — know what's going on, but not feel like I have an emotional stake in it," she replied. "Morgan's my friend, and I care, but she seems OK with whatever is going on between the two of them, so I need to be OK with it too."

"But you aren't," Tyler said wisely.

Kelsey took a deep breath, and decided to say what she had been holding in for a long time.

"I'm angry," she said simply. "Morgan is a wonderful person, and I feel like Bob has played with her emotions for too long. It troubles me, because you and I only see the good side of Bob, and it makes me feel like I'm misjudging him, because of what he's done to Morgan."

"What has he done?"

"He's made her feel worthless," Kelsey said, and for the second time that day, she felt tears coming to her eyes, this time for Morgan. "He won't marry her, he won't tell her why, and I'm sick of it. I won't give him the benefit of the doubt any more, but Morgan's decided to, and that makes me angry too."

Tyler quietly held Kelsey for a moment, and she wiped tears from her cheeks.

"I think you're right," Tyler said softly. "And that upsets me because I feel like I did the same thing to you."

Kelsey considered Tyler's words, then she spoke.

"No. It was different," Kelsey said firmly. "I knew why you wouldn't date me, and I knew that it had nothing to do with me. You never made me feel unimportant. In fact, I always knew just how important I was to you. So it's totally different. Morgan doesn't have that comfort, and I feel like she's letting him hang on to her because of what she can get for her family."

"Is that wrong?" Tyler asked.

"Actually, I've never asked myself that question," Kelsey admitted.

"At this point, Bob is helping Morgan's family, and Morgan's enjoying her life in San Francisco without him. Maybe it bothers you more than it's bothering her. Just because Morgan isn't stopping Bob from giving to her sisters doesn't mean that she feels like she owes him something."

"Maybe she feels like she's getting paid back," Kelsey said. She glanced at Tyler. "I'm not sure that I meant to say that out loud."

"I won't tell," Tyler said, kissing her.

"Do you understand him?" Kelsey asked Tyler.

"Mr. 'I've been married four times' ? I think not."

"See, that's another thing. He's been married four times, but he can't manage a fifth? And I don't even want Morgan to be his fifth wife," Kelsey sighed in frustration.

"I didn't realize that this was bothering you so much."

"I didn't either," Kelsey admitted.

"I'm sorry," Tyler said.

"For what? That Ryan invited Bob on our camping trip and Bob met Morgan there?"

"I feel like I should have warned Morgan, but this hasn't turned out how I expected either. I'm puzzled about why Bob let her walk away, when he won't let her go."

"That's an interesting way of putting it."

"It describes the situation. I know that Ryan has no clue about what's going on, or maybe he's in denial too."

"Or maybe nothing's going on. It's like you said, Bob's giving to Morgan's family, and she's allowing it, and that's all," Kelsey said.

"Maybe for Morgan, not for Bob."

"Maybe that's all that I care about," Kelsey said.

"Morgan?"

"Yes. Sorry, but I don't care about Bob's feelings."

"It's your right. You knew Morgan first. I'm glad she's OK, because I don't understand what's going on either."

Kelsey leaned her head on Tyler's chest, and he stroked her back.

"Your guests will arrive in fifteen minutes," the computerized voice of Athena announced.

"Athena, thank you," Kelsey said.

"No problem," Athena replied.

"Should we get ready? We can ponder Bob Perkins later," Tyler said.

"There's nothing to do," Kelsey said.

"You seem disappointed."

"I am. A little. But I appreciate what you did. I really overestimated my ability to make Thanksgiving dinner."

"Until you leave Simon and Associates, I don't want you volunteering to do anything else. It's too stressful for you. Promise me."

"I promise," Kelsey said solemnly. Tyler leaned down and kissed her.

Kelsey and Tyler spent the next fifteen minutes on the few last minute chores. Kelsey removed both cranberry and lingonberry sauce from the refrigerator, along with the deviled eggs and a crisp green salad. Margaret had made three different types of salad dressings, and Kelsey put those out as well.

As they worked, Kelsey gave Tyler lots of kisses. She knew that he was concerned about having dinner with both her father and Charles Jefferson, and she appreciated the fact that he was willing to brave them both during one meal.

Tyler removed the turkey from the oven seconds before the doorbell rang.

"Are you ready?" Kelsey asked Tyler as he placed the hot turkey on the large platter.

"As ready as I'll ever be," Tyler replied. Kelsey gave him another kiss.

"Let's go," Kelsey said happily, taking his hand and leading him to the front door of the house.

"Hi!" Grandma Rose said excitedly, giving Kelsey a hug.

"Hi, Grandma," Kelsey replied, hugging her back.

"It's good to see you," Charles Jefferson said to Tyler.

"You too, sir," Tyler replied, as Charlene Jefferson placed a pie plate into Tyler's hands.

"I made a chocolate pie for dessert," she said.

"Thank you," Tyler said.

"Did you bring your own apple pie, Dad?" Kelsey asked loudly.

"I brought your mother, so I did my part," Dan North replied.

"I made an apple pie for your father, Kelsey," Kelly North said, a tote bag in her hand.

"Come in, come in," Kelsey said to the group. "Let's have dinner."

Everyone washed up and settled into the dining room as Kelsey and Tyler took care of the last final touches. Kelsey sat down next to her grandmother as Tyler walked into the dining room, carrying the turkey on a large ornate platter. To Kelsey's great surprise, she realized that the beautifully-detailed seashore-inspired platter had been made by Peggy Schange.

"Let us give thanks," Papa Jefferson said. Everyone bowed their heads, and Tyler took Kelsey's hand under the table. "Thank you for allowing us to be together and to share in the earth's bounty on this beautiful day. We are grateful for the opportunity to welcome Kelsey and Tyler home, and we are thankful that they are happy, healthy, and safe. We are grateful for your love, and for your gentle reminder that although we have enough, there are others that need more, so on this day let each of us consider how we can be of service to others as we move forward in this year, and in years beyond. Thank you for your blessings. Amen."

"Amen," Everyone around the table echoed.

Kelsey lifted up the carving knife and fork. "Who will do the honors?" she asked.

"Tyler," Dan North said without hesitation. To Kelsey's ears, it sounded like a challenge, but undaunted, Tyler stood and took the utensils from Kelsey. As the rest of the table headed to the buffet with their plates and chatted, Kelsey watched in awe as Tyler expertly carved the turkey.

"Have you done this before?" Kelsey asked quietly, as he transferred slices of turkey breast onto the side of the platter.

"I learned from a video," Tyler replied.

"I see," Kelsey said in amusement.

As Tyler finished up, Grandma sat in her chair, her plate full of food.

"I'll take a drumstick, Tyler," she said.

"Here you go," Tyler said, transferring it to her plate. As people sat and Tyler placed turkey on their plates, Kelsey picked up her own plate and went to the buffet. It was incredible. Margaret had created a menu that combined Southern favorites, with Midwestern traditional foods, and a few added surprises. There was a plate of smoked salmon, and another of meatballs — both nods to Tyler's Norwegian heritage. Margaret and Ryan had made three kinds of rolls, including flaky biscuits. And in addition to the traditional Southern macaroni and cheese Kelsey had requested, there was a second pan of macaroni and cheese flavored with sausage, shrimp, and Cajun spices. Kelsey filled her own plate and headed back to the table.

Once Tyler had got food of his own and sat down next to Kelsey, Mama Jefferson turned to her.

"Kelsey, this is absolutely delicious. You did a wonderful job."

Kelsey was a little embarrassed. Although everything had clearly been organized on the table so that Kelsey could pass it off as her own work, Kelsey knew that she couldn't.

"Thanks, Mama, but I didn't cook. Tyler's chef did."

Kelsey watched as Charlene Jefferson, Kelly North, and Grandma Rose gave each other looks around the table.

"Oh, thank goodness," Kelly North said in relief.

"I told you that Kelsey wouldn't try to do all of this on her crazy work schedule," Mama said to Kelsey's mother.

"We were so worried," Kelly North said to Kelsey.

"I can't believe you talked Kelsey into doing this," Grandma Rose said to her son, gently swatting his hand. Dan North gave his mother a grin.

"She did great. I don't know what you're talking about," he said.

Kelsey glanced at her husband, and Tyler gave Kelsey a smile.

Everyone ate heartily and praised Margaret's work. Kelsey noticed that although her father had spoken to everyone else at the table, he seemed to be ignoring Tyler. It was clear that Tyler had noticed it as well. Papa was surprisingly quiet too.

"We're going to head on," Papa said, standing as dinner wound down.

"You aren't going to stay to watch the game?" Kelsey asked.

"We're going to go help with the free meal service downtown," Mama said, joining Papa.

"Can we get you some dessert?" Grandma asked.

"No, thank you, Mrs. North," Papa said to her.

"We have more pie at home," Mama added.

"Thank you for coming," Kelsey said, as she and Tyler stood to say goodbye to their guests.

"Thank you for the invitation. We'd love it if the two of you can join us on Saturday," Papa Jefferson said. Kelsey glanced at Tyler, who bit his lip. No wonder Papa had been quiet at dinner. He had been saving his comments for Tyler for Saturday.

"That would be very nice, thank you," Tyler said on the couple's behalf.

"Wonderful. We'll see you at six," Papa Jefferson said. Mama gave Kelsey a hug, and the Jeffersons left. Kelsey and Tyler sat back down at the table.

"What's for dessert?" Grandma asked.

Kelsey stood next to her father in the kitchen, getting out an ice cream scoop as he cut a large piece of Kelly North's apple pie for himself.

"How's married life?" he asked her.

Kelsey glanced at her father.

"That was random," she commented.

"I'd like an answer, Kelsey Anne," Dan North replied.

"Married life is fine," she said noncommittally.

"Fine?" her father asked in concern.

Kelsey gave him a smile. "I'm done teasing you. Married life is wonderful, and Tyler Olsen is the best husband on the planet."

"Do you mean that?"

"I do. Tyler is very kind, and I'm very happy."

"You seem happy."

"Do I?"

"You do. He's treating you well?"

"He couldn't treat me better," Kelsey replied.

"I doubt that, but I'll accept your answer," Dan North said, wiping off the knife and placing it to the side. "Have there been any problems?" he asked, pressing her.

Kelsey thought for a moment. "None I haven't caused," she replied. Her father laughed, and Kelsey grinned.

"Seriously, Kelsey. I'm your father. I'm concerned."

"I know, but you don't have to be. Tyler is the same as he always was. You made a good choice."

"Did I choose Tyler?" Dan North said in surprise, taking the offered ice cream scoop.

"You said I could marry him."

"Like you wouldn't have if I had said no," her father said, scooping out a large portion of ice cream.

"Are you really going to eat all of that?"

"I told you that I was worried about you."

"So you're going to drown your worries in vanilla bean ice cream?"

"That's the plan," Dan North said, setting the ice cream on top of the pie that was sitting in a bowl.

"You don't need to worry. Everything is fine."

"How's his mother?"

"Too busy to be concerned about us," Kelsey replied.

"Does Tyler come home on time?"

"Earlier than I do."

"So no problems?" he repeated.

"None."

Dan North looked at his only daughter. "You're telling me the truth."

"One hundred percent."

"So I can sleep at night?"

"You can."

"I can't," Dan North said. He lifted the ice cream scoop and put it back inside the container. He lifted a second large scoop of ice cream out, and placed it on top of the first. "Do you still love him?"

"Of course I do."

Dan North sighed. "I was afraid that you would say that."

"It's a bad thing to love my husband?" Kelsey asked.

"If you didn't, then you could come home."

"And you could lock me in my room and keep an eye on me twenty-four hours a day."

"Exactly," Dan North said unapologetically.

Kelsey giggled. "No. I love Tyler," she said.

"And he loves you?"

"Yes. Despite living with me for almost five months, he still does."

"You're a wonderful person. He'd be crazy not to."

"Thanks, Dad."

"I feel like I should ask you more questions, but I'm not sure what to ask to get a negative response from you."

"I don't have anything negative to say. Tyler's great. I love being married to him. He's thoughtful, way too generous, and wants nothing but the best for me."

"Now I don't believe you. No one is that great."

"Tyler is," Kelsey said firmly.

"Tell me one bad thing about him, then I'll stop," Kelsey's father said, picking up a spoon and taking a bite of ice cream.

Kelsey thought for a moment, then said, "He's used to having someone pick up after him, so he has a tendency to leave things around the house."

"Does he expect you to pick up after him?" Dan North asked sharply.

"No," Kelsey said.

Her father sighed and took another spoonful of ice cream. "Fine," he said. "How are you coping with the money?"

"Poorly," Kelsey admitted. "But I've been working a lot, so that allows me to ignore it."

"You said that he was too generous."

"He is. You should see our new house."

"I did. Your mother showed me the magazine article."

"She did?"

"Tyler's assistant sent it over. He thought she'd be interested."

"What did you think of it?" Kelsey said.

Dan North didn't answer, but instead took another bite of ice cream.

Kelsey watched him with a smile on her face. "He's a good man, Dad," she said.

"He'd better stay that way," her father said menacingly. Then he ate some more ice cream.

Kelsey and her father joined her mother, grandmother, and Tyler out in the backyard cottage. Kelsey cuddled on the love seat next to Tyler, her own bowl of dessert in her hands. Grandma was crocheting in a chair next to them, her partially-empty dessert plate on a side table. Kelly North looked at her husband as he sat down next to her on the sofa. He gave her an almost imperceptible nod.

Kelsey looked around the room curiously as the Lions game streamed on the television. It was just a little different than it had been in the summer, and she realized that the inside of the main house was different as well. When they had been in Port Townsend in July, the furnishings were casual, summery, and bright. But now that it was fall, it felt more cozy. Upholstered furniture had replaced the wooden chairs, there were soft blankets draped on the armrests, and it felt like a perfect place to snuggle, away from the cold fall air.

"Want a bite?" Kelsey asked Tyler, offering him a spoonful of cranberry cookie bar covered in vanilla bean ice cream.

"Yes," Tyler said, opening his mouth.

"It's delicious," Kelsey said, taking another bite of her own.

"You're delicious," Tyler whispered in her ear.

Kelsey blushed. "I'm surrounded by my family, Tyler," she said quietly.

"I hope to be surrounded by you soon," Tyler replied softly, kissing her neck.

At his words, Kelsey blushed scarlet. "I'm going to sit somewhere else," Kelsey warned. Tyler grinned and opened his mouth. Kelsey fed him another bite of dessert.

"Lions or Bears, Tyler?" Dan North asked. They were the first words that Kelsey's father had spoken to her husband all day.

"Bears," Tyler replied.

"Why?"

"The Lions have had too much drama lately," Grandma piped up.

"Is that your answer, Tyler?" Dan North asked.

"Yes," Tyler replied.

"That's fair," Dan North said. He turned back to his ice cream.

"What are you making, Grandma?" Kelsey asked.

"I thought that the two of you needed a blanket for your fancy new home," Grandma replied.

"Thanks, Grandma," Tyler said. Kelsey bristled just a little at the word 'fancy', but she knew it was true.

"I should be done by Sunday."

"It's OK if you aren't. It's not that cold yet," Kelsey said.

"I know, but I need to finish up my Christmas gifts before the holiday," Grandma said. She gave them a knowing smile, and Kelsey knew that Tyler had already told her about her cruise.

"Mom, you still haven't told us what you're doing at Christmas," Dan North commented.

"Now's a good time," Tyler said quietly to Kelsey. "She's going to Baja," he said to his father-in-law.

"Baja?" Kelly North asked.

"And Kelsey and I would like to send the two of you on a cruise around the Mediterranean," Tyler continued.

"What?" Dan North said. Kelly North looked at the couple in disbelief.

"It's fourteen days long, and you can leave after Christmas Eve," Kelsey piped up. She knew that her father would not want to miss the holiday shopping season at the store.

"We couldn't," Dan North said firmly.

"Of course you can, Danny," Grandma Rose said.

"No," Dan North said. He stood up abruptly and left the cottage.

"Give me a minute," Kelsey said to Tyler. She leaped up and followed her father into the backyard.

"You're going," Kelsey said to him.

Dan North gave her a hard look. He sat on the stairs leading back into the house.

"We aren't," he replied, as Kelsey sat next to him.

Kelsey sighed. "It's our gift to you, Daddy."

"It's Tyler's gift."

Kelsey flinched uncomfortably at her father's comment, but she pressed on.

"I'll pay for it out of my salary if that would make you feel better," Kelsey said in response. "I have the money."

Dan North surveyed his daughter. "No, that wouldn't make me feel better," he admitted.

"What's wrong with you?" Kelsey asked, but she suspected that she knew.

"It's a lot of things. Tyler has the financial means to give you anything you want, including buying you the building our store is located in. You're happy, which means the world to me, but also worries me, because you don't always know what's best for you. Your life with him is featured all over the media, and that concerns me."

"And?"

"And I'm terrified that I've let you down."

"Why? Because you're not a billionaire?"

"Maybe. Maybe it's also because I allowed you to marry one."

"Why would that be bad?"

"I'm worried about your values."

"You mean the cruise? We bought it at a charity auction."

"You mean Tyler bought it at a charity auction."

"Dad, part of the deal that I made with Tyler was to accept that now that we're married, our money is shared. In fact, according to Washington State law, everything we make is split 50/50."

"I know. I was married in Washington State too."

"So then you know that Tyler didn't buy it at a charity auction — legally we both did. I want you to have it as much as Tyler does. Maybe more."

"We can't accept that, Kelsey."

"You can't accept a gift from your daughter? Your daughter who loves you?" Kelsey said, leaning against her father's arm.

Dan North laughed. "You really want us to go?"

"I do. Consider it a partial payment for all of the terrible things I did as a child."

"You didn't do anything terrible," Dan North said.

"Let's go ask Mom. I bet she'll disagree with you," Kelsey replied.

"Probably. I hate this," Dan North said.

"What?"

"Worrying about you. Taking it out on Tyler."

"It's OK. He understands."

"I'm sure. Because he's such a great guy," Dan North snarled.

Kelsey burst out laughing. "Maybe we need to find you a therapist," she commented.

"Maybe. Are you sure that you're happy?"

"Blissful," Kelsey replied.

Her father stood up. "Fine. I'll go."

"And you'll have fun?" Kelsey asked, standing up.

"No promises," her father replied.

"You've been overruled, Danny," Grandma Rose said as Kelsey and her father re-entered the cottage. Kelly North was sitting and scrolling through pictures of the cruise ship on Tyler's Tactec tablet. "You and Kelly are going."

"I know. Kelsey told me," Dan North said, sitting back down. "Thank you both for the gift," he said, without a glance at Tyler.

"It's our pleasure, Dad," Kelsey said, sitting next to Tyler and holding his hand. Tyler gave her a smile.

Hours later, long after their guests had left, Kelsey lay in bed with Tyler, their hands intertwined. Kelsey was comfortable next to Tyler's warm body, and he lifted her hand to his lips and kissed it.

"I didn't expect that reaction," Kelsey said thoughtfully.

"Dan?" Tyler asked.

"Yeah."

"I did," Tyler replied.

Kelsey looked at him curiously. "Why?" she asked.

"You weren't born having issues with money," Tyler replied. "You learned them."

"OK, that's true, but what makes you say that? Have you and my father talked about money?" she asked.

"All the time," Tyler replied.

"What about it?" Kelsey asked.

"A lot of things. How my money affects you, how it affects our relationship. It's a big issue for him."

"I didn't know that," Kelsey said.

"Well, it's a big issue for you too," Tyler replied.

"I'm getting better," Kelsey pouted.

Tyler kissed her hand again. "You are," he replied.

"So what's Dad's problem?" Kelsey pressed.

Tyler was silent for a moment before he answered.

"He wants you to have a normal life, and he's angry that I can't give that to you," Tyler replied. "I don't blame him — I'm angry about that too."

"Don't be. I like our life," Kelsey replied.

"Do you?"

"Very much," Kelsey said.

"You don't miss your life before you had 24/7 security and paparazzi?"

"No, because before that, I didn't have you," Kelsey replied.

Tyler sighed. "I think Dan thinks that I tricked him. When we were at Darrow, I wasn't in the public eye. It wasn't until after we got engaged that the media paid attention to me. To us," he said.

Kelsey considered his words.

"I guess that's true. We were engaged, then we had the proxy fight, then the wedding, then Chris got hurt."

"It's been nonstop, and Dan's not happy about it. He thought things would be the same for you as they were when we were dating."

"I knew they wouldn't be," Kelsey said, stroking Tyler's chest.

"That's not an excuse I can use with your father."

"What does he want you to do?"

"Put the genie back in the bottle. Make the media go away."

"That's not going to happen," Kelsey scoffed. "It is what it is, and I'm fine with it. Dad's going to have to deal."

"I wish it wasn't like this," Tyler said.

"I know. But it is. We both knew that you wouldn't be able to have a truly private life once you joined Tactec. I love you, and this is all part of being with you."

"You really don't mind?"

Kelsey thought about the question before she answered it.

"I do sometimes. But I consider the alternative. Being without you isn't an option, so here we go," Kelsey said, stroking Tyler's chest again, "I don't blame you, because this isn't your fault. It's just a side effect of being Lisa Olsen's son. Anyway, it's not like I don't get anything out of this."

"You don't care about the money."

"Imagine if we were normal. You would work for a law firm downtown, just like I do. I would have promised to make Thanksgiving dinner, just like I did. And I would have been crying, with flour in my hair and an uncooked turkey in the oven at 11:55 this morning. So there are certainly some perks of the money I appreciate," Kelsey said sincerely.

Tyler laughed. "We just would have gone to a restaurant," he said.

"I know, but I wanted to have dinner here at home. That's another thing. I would have been crying in my parents' kitchen, not at this luxurious estate."

"It's a house."

"One we wouldn't have if you weren't Lisa Olsen's son. Think about it. There's all kinds of things that we have access to that make our day-to-day lives easier. Two cars, living downtown, Jeffrey. Jake doesn't have any of that. Most people don't. I'm grateful for it now."

"Sure, but you could live without it," Tyler said.

"Loop back to, 'I love you, and this is a part of my life with you,'" Kelsey said. "Dad will get over this."

"Will you?" Tyler asked.

Kelsey giggled. "One day," she replied.

"It all feels so normal to me," Tyler said. "I think that's part of the problem that Dan has with it. He thinks that I should be concerned."

"But you aren't, because you don't have any control over it?"

"I"m not, because in some ways I don't think it's a big deal."

"You weren't happy about the picture with Chris. Or your grades being leaked to the press," Kelsey pointed out.

"I don't like it when my private life is made public, but I don't care about the fiction that is written about us," Tyler replied. "Dan cares about both."

Kelsey understood Tyler's point. It was one thing to have the media breathlessly speculate about their lives — and an entirely different thing for their actual world to be spread over the internet.

"I don't know what you could do about it," Kelsey said. "People are interested in you."

"Actually, they are way more interested in you," Tyler said.

"I'm new to the family," Kelsey agreed.

"So you aren't upset?" Tyler asked.

"It's fine. Kelsey Olsen can post online about her new running shoes, and her favorite coffee shops, and the real Mrs. Tyler Olsen can cuddle in her husband's arms. That's fine with me."

"And the magazine articles that claim that you're miserably unhappy because I work all the time? That's fine with you too?"

Kelsey looked at Tyler in surprise. "Is that what they say?"

"We're getting divorced any day now," Tyler replied.

Kelsey laughed out loud. "No, we aren't."

"Obviously you don't read magazines," Tyler said.

"No, I avoid the newsstand. What else do I do?"

"You go shopping with Jess so the two of you can drown your sorrows under designer clothes, instead of dealing with your terrible marriages."

"Jess is miserable too, and she can't leave the cheating Ryan Perkins because she has kids?" Kelsey guessed.

"I thought you said that you didn't read magazines."

"I did before we got engaged. According to the media, Jess and Ryan's marriage has been on the rocks since the day we left Las Vegas," Kelsey replied.

"It's so ridiculous," Tyler said, "But Dan and Kelly have to deal with it."

Kelsey hadn't really thought about that issue. "I guess they do," she said.

"Dan told me that if you weren't happy, I'd better not step foot in Port Townsend, and I think he was a little surprised that I showed up," Tyler said.

"He was a little concerned," Kelsey noted. "But I told him the truth about how happy I am."

"Thank you," Tyler replied.

Kelsey giggled. "Maybe we should put my parents on a media diet."

"I don't think it would help, unless we put all of Port Townsend on it too."

"That's true, I'm sure our neighbors have plenty to share," Kelsey said. "They should all know better, though. Kelsey North isn't anything like the Kelsey Olsen in the press."

"Maybe they think you've changed," Tyler said.

"I haven't."

Tyler pulled Kelsey closer.

"I love being with you, and I don't care about what anyone thinks about us," Kelsey said. "You're mine. Always."

"That's good to hear," Tyler said. "I love you so much, and I just want you to be happy."

"I am," Kelsey said contentedly, snuggling against him.

Kelsey and Tyler woke up late the next morning, and stayed in bed even later. Finally, they got hungry, so they went down to the kitchen for breakfast.

"Leftovers?" Kelsey asked.

"Of course," Tyler replied.

"Even in a billionaire's house?" Kelsey teased.

"Even there," Tyler replied. "Remember, Lisa wasn't born rich."

"I know, but some people don't like leftovers."

"I do. So leftovers are fine."

"I'll heat them up for you," Kelsey said.

"You mean for us?"

Kelsey shook her head. "Actually, I'm going to make an omelet for myself. I'm not in the mood for leftovers right now."

Tyler laughed.

"What?" Kelsey pouted. "Do you think I'm spoiled?"

"No. You should eat whatever you want to eat. More leftovers for me," Tyler replied, giving her pouty lips a kiss.

Kelsey fixed a plate of leftovers for Tyler, and made a cheese omelet for herself. Tyler helped her carry the plates to the table, and they sat down. Kelsey reached over to Tyler's plate with her fork and took a small amount of his lingonberry sauce. She licked it off the fork and enjoyed the tangy taste.

"Margaret is really an incredible chef," Kelsey commented, cutting into her oozy cheese omelet.

"We're lucky to have her," Tyler replied.

"She seemed kind of upset," Kelsey said.

"She is. She really wants to know what's going on around there, but no one seems to know what's happening with either Lisa or Bob. The only person who isn't worrying Margaret is Ryan, and that worries her, because Ryan's always been the one whose life doesn't make sense. But right now, he's the stable person on the property."

"How about Jess and the twins?"

"Margaret thinks that Jess went back to work too early, that Allie cries too much, and that Rory cries too little."

"Maybe Margaret needs a vacation," Kelsey commented.

"She's going on one for the next two weeks."

"How will we eat?" Kelsey teased.

"Ryan and Katie will cook for us. Don't expect any meat now that Ryan's vegan."

"That's fine. Ryan's a great cook," Kelsey said. "It's so sad. That omelet was the first thing I've made in a while."

"You've been busy."

"Are you miserable because I work too much?" Kelsey teased.

"Yes."

"You are not."

"I am. You should quit."

Kelsey giggled.

"No," she said.

"Fine. I get you for the next three days, though. No work."

"No work?" Kelsey said. "I'm not sure that's allowed."

"We'll see about that," Tyler replied, kissing her.

A couple of hours later, Kelsey and Tyler headed out for a run. They ran up to Fort Worden Park, and enjoyed quite a few kisses on the now-empty field where they had got married just a few months earlier. On their way back home, they decided to make a short detour to Chetzemoka Park so Kelsey could have a ride on the swings.

When they turned on Jackson Street, Kelsey involuntarily glanced at a house that she knew quite well. She had spent hours, days, probably weeks in Eric Johns' house when she was a teenager — and the house kept secrets that Kelsey hoped to never share.

Kelsey looked away, feeling the uncomfortable feelings that she always felt when she passed by the house. Then, suddenly, a loud noise called her attention back. Two children, shouting and laughing, ran out the front door and dashed right in front of Kelsey and Tyler. Holding Kelsey's hand, Tyler deftly maneuvered around the children, and he continued to lead Kelsey towards the park.

Kelsey glanced back at the house. A woman stood on the porch, and the man next to her locked the front door. But to Kelsey's bewilderment, the man wasn't Eric.

A half-hour later, Kelsey sat on the bed in the master bedroom, her tablet on the bed in front of her. She was freshly showered and wrapped in a thick terry-cloth robe. A few minutes earlier she had declined Tyler's offer to join her in the shower, because she was overwhelmed by curiosity. The house on Jackson Street had been in the Johns family for at least three generations, maybe more. However, like Kelsey, Eric Johns was an only child, but Kelsey couldn't identify the man who had been locking the door of the house.

Kelsey looked at the tablet for a long moment, then picked it up and began typing. She reached the Jefferson County tax parcel search page in a flash. She typed in Eric's house number and street. She hesitated for just one moment, then tapped *search*.

When the parcel number appeared, Kelsey tapped again. She read the owner's mailing address in disbelief.

LTO Holdings, New York City.

Lisa and Tyler Olsen's property trust.

Kelsey looked through the page quickly, scanning the sections to find the sales information. She tapped on the slate gray bar, and the information appeared. LTO Holdings had paid more than a half-million dollars for Eric Johns' rundown bungalow. The sales date had been June 16, three weeks before her wedding.

Kelsey heard the water turn off in the bathroom, and she sat unmoving on the bed, the tablet in her hands. Kelsey knew that Tyler knew she would figure out what he had done — in fact, Kelsey thought that maybe he had wanted her to know. There were other trusts that Tyler could have bought the property with — Kelsey knew that for a fact. However, for this purchase, Tyler had chosen this trust, the one that Lisa had used to threaten Kelsey, the trust whose name Kelsey would never forget.

Kelsey closed the browser window and set the tablet back on the bed.

She wondered where Eric had gone. Kelsey was confident that he was no longer in Port Townsend. No one would have paid so much for Eric's house unless they were getting something else out of the deal. Especially not Tyler Olsen. Kelsey wondered if their deal allowed Eric to remain in Washington State. But Kelsey wasn't sure she should ask.

Because she didn't want to know.

Kelsey sighed deeply. A door to her past had been closed, by Tyler. Kelsey had mixed feelings. Relief was one, because Eric knew things about Kelsey that she didn't want to share. Although Eric had promised her that he would not tell her secrets, now Eric would be much less easy to find at a time when reporters continued to look for stories about the new Mrs. Tyler Olsen — and Kelsey had to admit that was a comfort.

Eric Johns had been Kelsey's friend. Her enemy. Her partner in crime. He had always been there, even when Kelsey wanted to forget that she had ever known him. And now he was gone. Paid off and removed from Kelsey's life without a trace, without so much as a goodbye.

And Kelsey was unable to name the feeling that accompanied that fact.

"I missed you," Tyler said, walking back into the master bedroom. One bright white towel was wrapped around his waist, as he dried his damp hair with another.

Kelsey looked into Tyler's sparkling eyes, and for a fleeting moment considered asking him for the truth. But instead, she said, "I missed you too." She held out her arms to her husband, so she could be wrapped in his warm embrace once more.

Hand in hand, the couple headed down Tyler Street towards downtown Port Townsend. It was cold and drizzly, as usual for that time of year.

Kelsey wore a bright red quilted down jacket, while Tyler wore his wool Filson jacket, a hand-me-down from Chris. Tyler also wore the hat and scarf that Kelsey had knit for him — which made her smile.

"So what wise words do you have for Ben today?" Kelsey asked.

"Hurry up and make more money so you can buy me out," Tyler replied.

Kelsey laughed. "Are you sick of Ben?" she asked.

"I don't have to deal with Ben, but he's certainly sick of me," Tyler replied. "You're sure that you don't want to be his partner?"

"Positive," Kelsey said. Tyler sighed, and Kelsey stroked his hand.

"Thank you for helping him," Kelsey said. In fact, Kelsey knew that — thanks to Tyler — Ben had become quite successful. Not only was the cafe serving breakfast, lunch, and dinner to large crowds, but Ben was even considering opening a second restaurant in town. However, Kelsey knew that the one concern Ben had about expanding was that, in order to do so, he would need to remain partners with Tyler. There was no way to pay Tyler back any time soon if Ben opened a second restaurant — and in fact, Ben might need more money from Tyler to expand.

"It's my pleasure, Princess."

"No it isn't," Kelsey pointed out.

Tyler gave her a grin. "I remind myself that I'm doing it for you. Because Ben is your friend."

Kelsey gave Tyler's arm a cuddle. "Not yours?"

"No. Ben and I will never be friends," Tyler said pointedly.

"Why?" Kelsey asked curiously.

"We're too different."

"That's probably true," Kelsey admitted. "What do you think of Ben's expansion idea?"

"What expansion idea?" Tyler asked her curiously.

"Ben hasn't talked to you about this?" Kelsey said in surprise.

"No. Ben wants to expand the restaurant?" Tyler asked.

Kelsey frowned. She had no idea that Ben hadn't discussed this with Tyler. She had heard about it from both Ben and her father in messages. Kelsey felt a little uncomfortable about being the first one to bring it up with Tyler, but now she didn't have a choice.

"Ben wants to open a second restaurant," Kelsey said.

Tyler laughed. "You're kidding."

"I'm not."

"He's barely got the first one under control," Tyler pointed out.

"He thinks that now could be a perfect time. He's got over six months to work out any issues before the summer season starts," Kelsey said.

"And how is Ben going to pay for a second restaurant?" Tyler asked Kelsey.

Kelsey gave him a smile.

"Is your job to convince me?" Tyler added.

"I didn't know Ben hadn't told you," Kelsey said, "But being that both he and my dad mentioned it to me, I'm guessing I'm supposed to play a part."

"Do you want me to help him?"

"I want you to listen to him," Kelsey said. "I'm OK with whatever decision you make."

"It's our money," Tyler pointed out.

"I don't know anything about being an angel investor," Kelsey said. "I'll trust your judgment."

"I can see I'm in this for the long haul with Ben," Tyler said.

"Do you mind?" Kelsey asked.

"No, but I think Ben's going to," Tyler replied.

A half-hour later, Ben sat down with Kelsey and Tyler. Kelsey was finishing her salad, while Tyler took the last few bites of his sandwich. Kelsey glanced at Ben. He was visibly nervous.

"So when are you buying me out?" Tyler asked Ben.

"I have a new business proposition for you," Ben replied, squaring his shoulders and looking at Tyler.

"Let's hear it," Tyler said, taking another bite.

"I want to open a second restaurant in town."

"I see," Tyler said, once he had finished chewing. It was clear that he wasn't going to make this easy for Ben. "What does that have to do with me?"

"I was hoping that you would invest," Ben replied. He glanced at Kelsey, and she nodded at him in encouragement. She knew that despite all appearances, Tyler was going to give Ben's idea a fair shot. Ben just had to keep talking.

"I see," Tyler repeated. "Why would I want to do that?"

"I think I could make you some more money," Ben said bluntly.

"I haven't seen a return on the money I've invested," Tyler replied.

"You will," Ben said.

"Tell me your idea," Tyler said.

"The restaurant in Kelsey's building is closing," Ben said hurriedly, as though Tyler might end the conversation. "I want to rent the space and open a new restaurant there."

"What kind?"

"A place for tourists to get a quick meal in the day, a small bistro at night."

"How is it different than here?"

"I'm thinking that it can be a little more upscale, with a higher price point," Ben replied.

"Will you have to buy equipment?"

"The current tenants are going out of the restaurant business. Dan thinks that they will sell me what's there for a good price," Ben replied.

"How much do you need?" Tyler asked. Kelsey smiled and Tyler gave her a wink.

"Thirty thousand," Ben said.

Kelsey looked at Ben in disbelief. That was twice what Tyler had invested previously.

"For what?" Tyler asked. He seemed less surprised than Kelsey.

"I'll need to hire at least two more people, and I want to make sure that I have enough in the bank for at least three months of rent."

"How much are you charging for a space in your building?" Tyler asked Kelsey. She shrugged.

"I have no idea," she said.

"Dan said that he'll charge me market rate," Ben said.

"No discount?" Tyler asked Kelsey. Ben looked at her.

"Hang on," Kelsey said, standing. "Let me talk to my dad."

A few minutes later, Kelsey left the North Wilderness Store to join Ben and Tyler on the sidewalk outside of the store. Instead of having Kelsey call her father, the trio had decided to walk down to Kelsey's building so Ben could show Tyler the space, while Kelsey spoke to her father.

"What did he say?" Tyler asked her.

"He said the rent was up to me," Kelsey replied. In fact, Kelsey's father had made a strong case for not giving Ben a discount for the lease — but ultimately, it was Kelsey's building.

Ben looked at Tyler.

"I'll loan you another twenty-five thousand. Work out a fair price with your landlord." Tyler said.

"Kels?" Ben said expectantly.

"I'll give you a 25% discount on the base rent," Kelsey said.

"Great!" Ben replied.

"But I want a percentage lease," Kelsey continued. "Five percent of all sales over ten thousand dollars per month."

Ben's mouth dropped open in surprise, and Tyler gave Kelsey a smile. She winked back at him this time. Her proposed lease meant that although Ben was getting a discount up front, he would have to pay her a percentage of sales. The more successful the business was, the more money she would receive.

"You probably should have known better than to negotiate with Kelsey," Tyler commented to Ben.

"I knew Kelsey before she went to law school. I didn't realize she had changed," Ben groused.

"It's a good deal," Kelsey said. "I could have asked for seven percent."

Ben was thoughtful for a moment, then he put out his hand. Kelsey shook it.

"Deal," Ben said.

"That was a surprise," Tyler commented as he and Kelsey headed toward the bookstore. Ben had left them to return to the cafe.

"Dad didn't want me to give him a discount," Kelsey replied. "This way, if he's successful, Ben will pay closer to market rate. So you think the new restaurant is a good idea?"

"I hadn't factored in the landlord's cut of the profits, but yes, I think Ben can make it work," Tyler said with a grin.

"You can have the building back at any time," Kelsey pointed out.

"It's yours," Tyler replied. "Stop trying to give it back to me."

"No," Kelsey commented.

Tyler leaned over and gave Kelsey a kiss. "The building is an important asset in your portfolio," Tyler said.

"I'm married to you, and we live in a community property state. I don't need a portfolio," Kelsey said sassily. But despite her bold words, she knew that she did. Everyone should have money of their own. Even a billionaire's wife.

"I know you don't mean that."

"Fine. My portfolio is large enough," Kelsey clarified. "I have real estate, stocks, cash, and jewelry."

"Jewelry isn't part of your portfolio," Tyler said.

"You've bought me a lot of diamonds."

"I've bought you diamonds because it was a way of transferring assets to you before we were married, and you need jewelry to wear now that we are. Diamonds are a terrible investment."

"I have to keep the building?"

"You do," Tyler said firmly. "I want your money to rival mine."

"I don't think that's going to happen," Kelsey said dismissively.

"Who told me that she wanted to be the next Lisa Olsen?" Tyler asked.

Kelsey sighed. "I did."

"Don't give up your dreams just because you married me," Tyler warned.

"I won't," Kelsey said.

"Good. Because I want you to become a billionaire too."

"You do?" Kelsey asked, glancing at him.

"Of course I do," Tyler said, brown eyes sparkling. "If you become a billionaire, I'll get half the money. We live in a community property state," he teased.

Kelsey giggled. "Yeah, because you need more money," she said sarcastically.

"Who doesn't?"

"Tyler, there are some things that money can't buy."

Tyler kissed the top of her hair.

"The most important things," he agreed.

"Exactly," Kelsey said, giving his arm a cuddle. "Thank you for coming here with me," she said.

"I wouldn't be anywhere else," Tyler replied.

At the bookstore, Kelsey browsed the investing section. In the back of her mind, Kelsey had always wanted to start her own business like Lisa Olsen — and ever since Kelsey had been with Tyler, she knew that she wanted to start it with her own money. Thanks to her thrift and lack of expenses, Kelsey's student loans had been paid off — and because of Tyler's generosity, Kelsey no longer needed to spend a dime of her salary from Simon and Associates. It was transferred automatically from her bank account into a money market fund. Kelsey knew that she needed to learn more about investing, not only for her own money, but also to understand Tyler better.

As Kelsey picked up a book about real estate investing, she remembered something that she thought she had put out of her mind. Eric's house.

When she had been online, looking up the owner, Kelsey was confident that she didn't want to know the details of what Tyler had done. She had felt overwhelmed with emotions that she couldn't describe, and that had made her uncomfortable.

But after the lunch with Ben, and the discussion of investments with Tyler, Kelsey felt a little more secure. Now she felt as though she could discuss Eric's house with Tyler as just another investment. As a lawyer, Kelsey knew how to separate feelings from fact and emotions from actions. And she thought she could use those skills to find out what she wanted to learn from Tyler.

But as they left the bookstore, a bag full of books in one of Tyler's hands, Kelsey felt emotion creep back in, just as it always had when she thought about Eric. And as she invariably did, Kelsey spoke her mind, without concern of the potential risk.

"So is Eric allowed to come back to Port Townsend?" Kelsey asked Tyler.

"Why do you want to know?" Tyler asked, and the question surprised Kelsey.

"I guess I'm wondering how good of a negotiator you are," Kelsey replied.

"Good answer. Yes, Eric can return any time he would like to, but he'll need a new place to stay. I only bought the house. He's the one who decided to go."

Kelsey frowned. "Don't lie to me, Tyler. That house isn't worth half of what you paid for it. It wasn't just a real estate sale."

"I didn't lie to you. I merely suggested to him that I might be inclined to pay more depending on how many miles away he decided to move."

"Based on the purchase price, I'm assuming he moved to Antarctica."

"Actually, I believe he chose Mexico."

"You know where he is?" Kelsey asked as they turned up Quincy Street.

"I could find him. Do you need to talk to him?"

"No."

"I wondered how long it would be before you asked me."

"I just found out."

"When we passed by the house?'

"Yes." Kelsey surveyed Tyler. "Why did you buy it?" she asked.

Tyler sighed. "Because I want to protect you."

"Eric wasn't going to talk," Kelsey said.

"The numbers that he was being offered were getting larger, Kelsey," Tyler replied.

"How do you know?"

Tyler was silent for a moment.

"Because I was one of the people offering him money to talk," he finally replied.

Kelsey looked at her husband in disbelief. She felt a catch in her throat as she asked, "What do you want to know?"

Tyler pondered her. "Will you tell me?" he asked.

Kelsey looked away from him. "No," she whispered.

"Then let's leave it," Tyler said unconcernedly.

"No, let's not," Kelsey said in a rush. "Ask me your question. I'll answer it."

"You don't have to," Tyler said.

"I know," Kelsey replied. She felt tears coming to her eyes. She had kept so many secrets, and they were starting to weigh on her.

They paused on the quiet street in front of Memorial Field. Tyler gently wiped a tear away from her eye with his finger.

"What are you afraid of, Kelsey?" he asked.

"That you won't love me," she said softly.

"I will always love you," Tyler replied.

"Then why do you want to know what I've done?" Kelsey asked. "If not to judge me?"

Tyler was thoughtful, and for a moment, they stood in their shared silence.

"I want to know if you loved him," Tyler finally said. "I want to know why he had such a large impact on your life. I've known a lot of people, and not one of them have had the effect on my life as you have had on mine. But I don't think that the reverse is true. I want to know what Eric Johns meant to you."

Kelsey heard a tone in Tyler's voice, one she had heard before.

"Are you jealous?" she asked.

"There is no word in the English language that can convey the intense jealousy I feel," Tyler replied.

Kelsey considered telling Tyler not to be jealous about Eric, but before the words escaped, she paused. That was not what Tyler wanted to hear.

"You aren't jealous," Kelsey concluded. "You're envious."

"What's the difference?" Tyler snapped.

Kelsey ignored his anger, because she felt it had nothing to do with her. She could tell that Tyler's emotions were getting the best of him. Eric had that way with people, even now, when he was thousands of miles away.

"You know I'm not interested in Eric now. Even if he was standing right here, you know that I would choose you. So you can't be jealous. You think that Eric had a relationship with me that is more intense than the one that you have with me, and you envy him for that," Kelsey replied.

"No, I don't think. I know that your relationship was more intense with him than it is with me, and I want to know why," Tyler replied.

"Intensity is not always good, Tyler," Kelsey replied.

"I don't care. I want to understand," Tyler replied.

Kelsey nodded thoughtfully. "OK," she said. "I owe you an explanation. You promise that you won't judge me?"

"I promise," Tyler said. "I just want to know the truth."

"My truth? Because it's probably different than Eric's," Kelsey said.

"All I care about is you, and how you felt," Tyler said.

"Fine," Kelsey said. She took Tyler's hand, and placed it inside her own. She could feel him relax, and as he did so, she belatedly realized that Tyler might have wanted to know about her relationship with Eric for a long time, ever since they had run into him at the grocery store.

"I thought I was in love," Kelsey said softly. "I thought that was how love felt. Eric knew that it wasn't love, but he enjoyed watching me struggle with him, and with the world, because that's the kind of person he is. He's an observer. He'll let you live your life, and he'll live his. He'll join in when it's fun, and walk away when it's not." Kelsey felt a tear roll down her cheek. "Drunk teenage girls are fun to watch," she said.

Tyler put his arm around Kelsey's shoulders, and she continued.

"I didn't know what I was doing, or why I was doing it. I just did it. And because Eric was there through all of those experiences, I link him to the feelings I felt at the time. None of those feelings are good, Tyler, but they were very intense.

"So when I see Eric, or talk to him, or even think about him, I think of those moments, and those feelings. The feelings of being alone and afraid. The rush of anxiety when you're about to do something you know is stupid, but you also know you're going to do it anyway. Eric was a spectator — at most he was the person I projected my feelings onto. He witnessed me at my worst, and I guess in some ways encouraged me in my excesses.

"But he never saw the true Kelsey," she said, looking into her husband's eyes. "He saw the scared little girl, fueled by alcohol. I saved the real Kelsey for you. You get the fussy, grumpy, complaining Kelsey, who is the person I really am."

Tyler smiled at her words, and Kelsey continued.

"Eric's version of Kelsey is like the Kelsey Olsen on Instagram. She seems real, but she's really a poor reflection of who I am, and how I think. Sometimes it's right, but usually it's not, and occasionally it's completely wrong. That's the Kelsey that Eric knows. There's no reason to envy him. Because the real Kelsey is right here, and you have the real me."

Kelsey looked at Tyler, and at his smile, and she knew she had said the right thing. She had told him her truth, and by telling him, she had told herself as well. Until this moment, Kelsey had never analyzed her relationship with Eric, because it had always felt so shameful, because of her actions during their time together. But after this conversation, Kelsey knew, perhaps for the first time, that she was truly free of her time with Eric.

A warm fire crackled in the living room fireplace. Kelsey and Tyler lay together on the sofa, wrapped in each other's arms. Tyler kissed Kelsey on the neck, and Kelsey pulled him closer. They were both fully clothed, but Kelsey knew that wouldn't last long. She pressed against him and Tyler blissfully sighed. Then the doorbell rang.

They both paused, quiet as they lay together. The doorbell rang again.

"You aren't expecting anyone, are you?" Tyler asked, getting off the sofa and standing up.

"No," Kelsey said.

"I guess everyone knows that you're in town," Tyler said. "I'll see who it is."

Kelsey looked into his eyes, then let her eyes travel down his body. She gave him a meaningful glance. Tyler looked down at his own body, and adjusted himself. Kelsey giggled.

"This better not take long," Tyler commented as Kelsey stood up. He headed for the door. Kelsey pulled her shirt down and followed him. She was curious about who was ringing their bell, and thought that she needed to be at the door to identify the person, since Tyler didn't know that many of her neighbors.

Tyler opened the door. Grandma Rose stood on the porch, her small piece of luggage next to her.

"Grandma," Tyler said in greeting, but Grandma Rose seemed preoccupied as she rolled her luggage into the house.

"I'm moving in," Grandma said without preamble.

Kelsey looked at Tyler helplessly.

"Let me take that for you, Grandma," Tyler said, taking the luggage from her hand. "I'll put it upstairs for you."

"Thank you, Tyler," Grandma Rose said.

Tyler lowered the handle, picked up the luggage, and walked off, closing the front door as he did so.

"Grandma, what happened?" Kelsey said. She could tell that her grandmother was quite upset.

But instead of answering, Grandma Rose just sighed.

A few minutes and a mug of cocoa later, and Grandma had related her latest fight with Kelsey's mother to the couple. Kelsey called her father, who was relieved to know that his mother was safe, as she had stormed out of the North house while he had been in his storage shed.

"We're happy to have you stay with us," Tyler said to Grandma as Kelsey walked back into the kitchen.

"I'm glad that someone is," Grandma Rose said, swirling the last of the cocoa in her cup.

"Do you need anything else, Grandma?" Kelsey asked. "Another cup of cocoa?"

"I'm fine, dear," Grandma Rose said. "I'll just sit in the living room and work on your afghan." She stood up from her seat at the kitchen table, and picked up the large tote bag she had carried into the house. "Get back to whatever you were doing. Pretend I'm not here," she added as she headed to the living room.

Tyler and Kelsey glanced at each other.

"We'll be upstairs," Tyler said, brightly, taking Kelsey's hand, and pulling her out of the kitchen.

Tyler shut and locked the door of their bedroom, as Kelsey lay on the bed. Tyler turned and smiled at her.

"So let's get back to what we were doing," he said, climbing into bed next to her. He kissed Kelsey's neck again, but Kelsey didn't react.

"Do you think that Grandma can hear us?" she asked him.

"No," Tyler said, nuzzling Kelsey.

"I wonder what she thinks about us being up here alone," Kelsey mused.

Tyler broke away from Kelsey. "Are you serious?" he asked her.

Kelsey frowned. "It's a little weird, right?"

"We could be doing anything up here," Tyler pointed out. "Maybe we were reading, or playing a game before she got here."

"Suppose she knocks?"

"She won't."

"How do you know?" Kelsey challenged him.

"I sense that the mood is gone," Tyler said thoughtfully. "Hopefully, Grandma Rose will go to bed soon."

"She's a light sleeper," Kelsey said in reply.

Tyler surveyed his wife. "Are you saying that you won't sleep with me while your grandmother is in the house?"

"We can sleep," Kelsey said.

Tyler gave Kelsey a hard look. "You know what I mean, Kels. Have sex," Tyler replied.

"Your bride is shy," Kelsey said, echoing Tyler's previous comments.

Tyler leaned back on his pillow. Then he sat up.

"Come with me," he said to her, standing up.

Surprised, Kelsey scrambled after him as he left the bedroom. They walked downstairs, and Kelsey followed Tyler to the living room. Grandma was sitting in front of the fireplace, afghan in her hands.

"Kelsey and I are going out," Tyler said. "Do you need us to bring anything back?"

"No, dear, I'm just going to sit here and crochet," Grandma replied.

"OK, we'll be back in a bit," Tyler said, walking over to the door, and handing Kelsey her fleece jacket.

"Where are you going?" Grandma asked.

"Port Hadlock," Tyler said, putting on his own jacket.

"Have fun. See you later," Grandma said, as Tyler opened the front door.

"Bye, Grandma," Kelsey said as they left. She and Tyler walked down the porch stairs.

"What's in Port Hadlock?" Kelsey asked.

"I have no idea," Tyler said.

"Then why are we going there?" Kelsey asked.

"We aren't," Tyler said, opening the door to the car for Kelsey.

"Then where are we going?" Kelsey asked him, completely confused as she got into the car.

"We have business to attend to," Tyler replied, closing the car door firmly.

Kelsey looked into her husband's brown eyes, and stroked his face. Completely relaxed and blissful, she smiled at him sleepily. Tyler kissed her lips.

"You can't fall asleep here, Princess," he said. "We have to go back."

"No," Kelsey teased, putting her arms around his neck. "I want to see you explain to Grandma why we've been gone for three hours, when Port Hadlock is a twenty-minute drive away."

Tyler laughed. "I should have said we were driving to Sequim. That's an hour and a half round trip."

"It wouldn't have worked," Kelsey said, kissing him. "She would have asked for something that you can only buy at Walmart, then we would have been in trouble."

"We would have told her that whatever she wanted was sold out," Tyler said, kissing his wife's cheek.

Kelsey laughed delightedly. "You're good," she said. "You should have been here when I was in high school. I bet I would have never been caught doing anything."

"I'm happy to be here now," Tyler said, pulling her closer.

"Me too," Kelsey said happily. She looked around at the simply-decorated hotel room where Tyler had brought them. "Can I ask you a question?"

"Absolutely."

"Why didn't we just go to the Airstream trailer?" she asked. The trailer, which they had used for their wedding, was still parked next to the house.

"Would that have been far enough away from your grandmother?" Tyler asked.

Kelsey was thoughtful. "Maybe not," she admitted.

"Anyway, Patrick's there, so I would have had to throw him out," Tyler added.

"Patrick's in Port Townsend?" Kelsey asked. Patrick was the Tactec security person assigned to protect Kelsey's family on the Olympic Peninsula. "I thought he lived in Port Angeles, near Grandma."

"He does, but Grandma's here now. He drove her over, and he's taking advantage of the weekend to check on your family in Gig Harbor. But he's staying in the trailer tonight."

"I had no idea," Kelsey said, cozy in Tyler's arms.

"Why would you?"

"There's just a lot that goes on behind the scenes when it comes to Security. In everything in your life, really," Kelsey said.

"Our lives," Tyler corrected. "If you're interested, Jeffrey will update you."

"It's not necessary," Kelsey said, closing her eyes and cuddling against Tyler's bare chest. "I just need to know where you are."

Tyler kissed her hair. "Right here. With you," Tyler replied.

Before they drove back to the house, they swung by the grocery store to pick up ice cream, as an excuse for their long trip away.

As they headed back into downtown Port Townsend, they drove past the North Wilderness Store, and Kelsey spotted the beautifully-decorated windows of her parents' shop. For the second year in a row, she hadn't been in Port Townsend to help.

There had been a time in the not-so-far-away past when Kelsey wouldn't have cared. She had been focused on herself, not on her family. Even when she had been in college, and perhaps up to entering Darrow Law School, Kelsey had been dedicated to her own dreams. But ever since she had met Tyler, Kelsey had started to see how intertwined life was with work. Tactec had started as a family business too.

After talking with Ben, Kelsey had realized that during this weekend she probably needed to check in with her parents, and find out how their business was doing this year. The North Wilderness Store had been her father's dream, and Kelsey wanted to know if it was still.

Kelsey and Tyler woke up the next morning, once again wrapped in each others' arms.

"Good morning," Kelsey said, as Tyler looked at her with his sparkling brown eyes.

"Good morning, Princess," Tyler said, kissing her deeply. He broke away and added, "Don't worry, I won't start anything. I know your grandmother is here."

Kelsey giggled, and kissed Tyler's cheek. His stubble tickled her lips. "I guess we need to make a trip to Sequim later," she said.

"Just say the word," Tyler replied, kissing Kelsey's collarbone.

"Hey, I thought you weren't going to start anything," Kelsey protested.

"Is kissing you starting something?"

"Being within five feet of me is starting something."

Tyler laughed. "Well, that's a problem because I sleep in the same bed as you."

"See, you're starting something," Kelsey teased. Tyler pulled her closer as they lay under the sheets. Kelsey had on pajamas, and Tyler was wearing pajama pants as a concession while Grandma Rose was staying with them.

"I love you so much," Tyler said, stroking her face.

"Do you?" Kelsey asked.

"I do."

"I love you too. Thanks for coming to Port Townsend with me." With all their interactions involving Ben, Charles Jefferson, Kelly North, and Dan North — plus the added surprise of Grandma Rose's arrival — Kelsey felt she owed Tyler thanks, if not an apology.

"I'd go anywhere with you," Tyler replied. Kelsey knew this to be true. On Wednesday night, Tyler had not only been in Bill Simon's office, he had been working for him, just to make sure that Kelsey was able to leave.

"I know," Kelsey said, cozying up to him. She felt his gentle breathing. "What should we do today?" she asked.

"Anything but play Scrabble," Tyler replied.

Kelsey laughed. "I could ask Grandma to let you win," she commented.

"Maybe," Tyler said, laughing with her. "I love when you laugh."

Kelsey looked at him seriously. There was something that she wanted to tell him, and now was the right time. "You know how happy I am to be with you, right?" she asked. "Anyone who thinks I'm not doesn't know me."

"Including Dan?"

"My father needs to stop reading the tabloids," Kelsey said. "All he had to do was ask me."

"That's all I want, you know," Tyler said. "I just want you to be happy."

"I couldn't be happier," Kelsey said, stroking his bare chest.

"Not at all?"

"No," Kelsey said.

"OK," Tyler replied.

"Do you believe me?" Kelsey asked.

Tyler was thoughtful. He nuzzled her hair and stroked her back. "Sometimes."

"When don't you?" Kelsey pressed.

"My whole life, I've been defined by the money that my mother has. So sometimes it's a little unbelievable to me that there are people who love me just for being me."

Kelsey held Tyler close. She felt a pang of sadness for him.

"You know that there are people like that, though," Kelsey said. "Me, your family, my family, your friends. We don't care about the money."

"I know. That's part of the reason I like to come here. I'm just another person. And that's something I love about you."

"But?"

"I don't know, Kelsey. I guess the media is starting to get to me too. They know all the right buttons to press to make me feel insecure."

"They don't know anything about us," Kelsey pointed out.

"I know, but I don't spend as much time with you as I wish I could, and I wonder what you think about us."

"It should be obvious, but you could ask me."

"What do you think about us?" Tyler asked, kissing her hand.

"I think that somehow I managed to find the kindest, most loving husband on the planet, and everyday I wonder what I did to be so blessed," Kelsey said honestly. "You have no idea what you mean to me, and maybe that's my fault, because I'm too busy enjoying being with you to tell you how much I love you."

"You really think that?"

"I do," Kelsey said firmly.

"Do you always promise to be honest with me? That you'll tell me if something's not right?"

Kelsey giggled. "I'm pretty sure I already do that."

Tyler smiled at her, but said, "Promise me."

"I promise," Kelsey said. "You're a wonderful husband, Tyler."

"You're a wonderful wife."

"Thank you," Kelsey said, editing herself, because she knew that Tyler didn't like it when she put herself down. Like Tyler, she sometimes also felt insecure, but unlike him, she didn't always feel secure enough to share her feelings.

"The best moment in my life was when I sat next to you in class," Tyler said.

Kelsey smiled at his words. That had been so long ago, and so many things had happened between that moment and the one they were sharing now.

"The best moment in my life is this one," Kelsey said as she gave him a kiss.

Tyler and Kelsey walked hand-in-hand down to the kitchen. The smell of freshly-cooked bacon hit their noses just before they walked inside.

"Good morning, Grandma," Kelsey said. "You didn't have to cook."

"It's my pleasure, dear."

"Thanks, Grandma," Tyler said to her.

"I know that you kids got in late. How was Port Hadlock?" Grandma asked as she flipped a pancake. Tyler and Kelsey smiled at each other.

"It was fine," Kelsey replied. "We didn't wake you when we came in, did we?" she asked. The house had been quiet when the couple had returned the previous night, and they hadn't seen Grandma Rose.

"Nope. I slept like a log," Grandma said, placing a warm pancake on a plate. Kelsey sat down at the kitchen table in her pajamas, while Tyler walked over to the refrigerator. He had put on his Portland State sweatshirt.

"Can I help with anything, Grandma?" Tyler asked.

"I've got it under control, thanks, Tyler," Grandma said, flipping another pancake onto the plate. "You can take the maple syrup out of the fridge, though."

"OK," Tyler said.

"What do you kids have planned today?" Grandma asked. "I don't want to get in your way."

"You won't," Kelsey replied. "We're going to the Jeffersons' for dinner tonight, and I thought I'd teach Tyler how to make cookies."

"We might take a drive later," Tyler said meaningfully to Kelsey.

"Right, of course," Kelsey said, suppressing a giggle.

"I guess this is your first vacation in a while," Grandma mused, as she put the last of the pancakes on the plate. "How is your father doing, Tyler?"

"He's doing much better," Tyler said.

"When did you last speak to him?" Kelsey asked. Because Tyler usually called Chris from work, he didn't always remember to mention it to Kelsey.

"Tuesday," Tyler replied. "He said that he was working on our Christmas gift."

Kelsey looked at Tyler in puzzlement. "Chris is making a gift for us?"

Tyler shrugged. "That's what he said. He also said that he was sending something for me to give to Lisa."

"OK, that's weird," Kelsey editorialized.

"Chris is weird," Tyler replied.

"Is he walking yet?" Grandma said, directing Tyler to pick up the plates of pancakes. He did so, and carried them over to the table.

"He said that he can walk to the door of his room without help, and down the corridor of the center with a walker. So he's improving."

"That must be very hard for him," Grandma said, picking up the maple syrup and joining the couple at the table. She and Tyler sat down.

"He's just focusing on getting better," Tyler said.

"I'm glad that you and Kelsey were able to spend some time with him. I'm sure that he appreciated it."

Tyler gave Kelsey a look. Like Tyler, Kelsey wasn't sure whether Chris appreciated their visit or not. Of course they had been able to help with the gallery and the doctors, but it had been a very emotionally difficult time for them all.

"I hope so," Tyler said diplomatically.

"Dig in," Grandma said, picking up her fork.

After breakfast, Tyler and Kelsey got dressed and headed out for a walk. Kelsey felt Tyler's warm hand next to her own as they strolled in the crisp fall air. Kelsey felt so happy. Despite the small dramas, being in Port Townsend this time felt perfect to her. She was with her husband, and she knew how much he cared for her, because he had been willing to share his vulnerabilities with her.

Tyler's conversation with Grandma Rose about Chris had been emotionless and to the point. It was the side that Tyler presented to the world, that of a man firmly in control of his feelings and of everything else. But like Tyler saw the real Kelsey, Kelsey knew that she saw the real Tyler. A man with passion. And Kelsey knew that was a side that Tyler only shared with her.

"So where are we going?" Tyler asked Kelsey.

"Where is there to go?" Kelsey teased.

"There are things to do in Port Townsend," Tyler pointed out.

"Let's go to the lagoon. We haven't walked there in a while," Kelsey replied.

"Is your grandmother OK? I was surprised that she didn't want to join us," Tyler commented. They had invited her, but Grandma had said that she would remain at home.

"I think she's serious about finishing the afghan," Kelsey replied. "Don't worry, she's like me. She'll let you know what she wants."

Tyler laughed. "I guess that trait runs in the family."

"It does. Wait until we have kids."

"Are you thinking about that?" Tyler asked.

"Not yet."

"Good," Tyler replied.

Kelsey looked at him, a little surprised. "I thought you were ready for children at any time," she commented.

Tyler considered his words before he spoke. "I think I'm still trying to figure out Chris, which is why I said that," Tyler explained. "Whenever you want to have kids is fine with me. I'll have nine months to figure out how to be a father."

Kelsey stroked the back of Tyler's hand with her thumb. "What's bothering you? You'll be as great of a father as you are as a husband."

"That's what's bothering me," Tyler quipped.

Kelsey frowned. "What did I tell you? You're awesome."

Tyler ran his hand through his hair. "What do you think makes a good parent?" he asked her.

"Love. Caring for your children," Kelsey said.

"So why is Chris so terrible at that?" Tyler asked.

"I think he loves you," Kelsey said. "But I think he missed the part about how to care for your child."

"What do you think that means?" Tyler asked.

"It means you put your child's needs first," Kelsey said.

"Is it that simple? What about self-care? What if there's a conflict between the two?" Tyler asked her.

"I guess you have a point," Kelsey said. "OK, how about this, a good parent weighs their desires against their child's needs and balances the two."

"Chris did that," Tyler said. "I lost."

"This was supposed to be an easy question," Kelsey commented.

"I thought so, too," Tyler said. "I'm just trying to pin down why Chris failed."

"To make sure you don't fail?" Kelsey asked wisely.

"Yes," Tyler replied.

Kelsey knew that Tyler wouldn't fail, that he would be a wonderful father, but she also knew that Chris's example haunted him. Tyler would never allow himself to be like Chris, but he wanted to know what had gone wrong for his own comfort.

"I think Chris underestimated how much you needed him," Kelsey concluded. "I think that he thought he could be a part-time parent, and maintain his relationship with Cherie. That's why he chose to leave."

"Then Lisa shut him out completely," Tyler mused.

"Right. I think Chris didn't know what to do once you were back in his life. He couldn't pick up where he had left off, because too much time had passed. Then after the lawsuit, and after you found out about Cherie, Chris lost his moral standing with you. He knows that, so he's doubling down on the decisions that he made before, so he doesn't feel guilty about ruining his relationship with you. He can make you the problem, instead of thinking about himself and his actions."

Tyler was quiet as he thought. "You're very insightful," he finally said to her.

"I try," Kelsey replied. Tyler lifted her hand to his lips and kissed it. "You won't make those mistakes, Tyler," she added.

"I know," Tyler said.

"Do you?"

"I think I do. For one, I'm in love with the woman who will be the mother of my children. Chris didn't have that."

"No, I guess he didn't," Kelsey said. It was clear from everything that Chris had said that his marriage to Lisa was not out of love on Chris's part, but because of their baby, Tyler.

"What kind of person makes that choice?"

"The choice to leave their family? A person like Chris," Kelsey shrugged.

"That's what I don't understand."

"Because he's your father. And you can't believe that your father could make that kind of choice."

Tyler stopped on the sidewalk and looked at Kelsey. She could tell that her words had had an impact. "You're brilliant," Tyler said.

"Thank you," Kelsey said.

"That's the problem. I feel like my father could not make that kind of choice, because what would that mean about me?"

"So you don't want to believe that Chris is that kind of person," Kelsey said. "You want to believe that you must be misunderstanding something about him."

"But I know I'm not. He is that way. He made those choices."

"That's him. That's not you. You may be Chris's son, but that's all. You're nothing like him, at least not in the ways that matter."

Tyler nodded thoughtfully. They began walking again.

"I needed you to help me see that," he said to her. "It's funny. At work, I wish I was more like Lisa, because I think it would be easier to be CEO, but at home, I fear being like Chris."

"You are your own person. Your parents don't define you. I guess that's easy for me to say, though. I don't have famous parents."

The couple walked in silence for a few moments as they crossed over to the lagoon. Kelsey knew that Tyler was pondering her words.

"You've been thinking a lot this vacation," Kelsey commented.

"I have a lot to think about, and this is the first time I've had time to deal with the questions on my mind," Tyler replied.

"Is there anything else on your mind?"

"Well, when I was in treatment, my therapist said that there were four people that were important in my life. We've dealt with Chris, you've said that you're OK. So I guess that leaves Lisa and Ryan."

"What do you think about them?" Kelsey asked curiously.

"I don't want to think about them," Tyler replied. "It's too much for one day," he added with a smile.

Kelsey giggled. "Come on, tell me," she coaxed.

"I figure that I can deal with whatever Lisa has planned when we're at her house for Christmas," Tyler said. "And I'm just going to keep avoiding Ryan. So, problems solved."

"What does Lisa have planned?" Kelsey asked. She couldn't control her curiosity.

"Lisa's figured out my new job," Tyler said. "I know, because Bob mentioned that it was his job to train me for it, but I don't know what my actual title is going to be. I'll know by the annual meeting."

"She thinks you're ready," Kelsey said.

"Yes."

"Does that worry you?"

Tyler was thoughtful. "I think I can handle it," he concluded.

"You're confident."

"I've seen how Lisa and Bob run the company for a while. It seems confusing from the outside, but now I'm starting to get it."

"So you think you're ready to be CEO?"

"No. But I think I'm ready for the first step to getting there."

"I'm proud of you," Kelsey said. She knew that, ever since Lisa had floated the idea of Tyler becoming CEO, he had been unsure of his ability to take on the role. His confidence made Kelsey feel as though he had moved past some of his doubts.

"It's thanks to you."

"It isn't."

"It is. Being with you makes me feel like I can do anything," Tyler said and Kelsey beamed. He kissed her hand again.

"Flatterer," Kelsey said, and Tyler put his arm around her shoulders. "So that's all you have to say about Lisa?"

"For now," Tyler said. "I need to deal with Chris before I can deal with Lisa again. I need to know how much of my childhood I can blame her for."

Kelsey laughed, and Tyler gave her a smile.

"What about Ryan?"

"What about him?"

"He's person number four on your list."

"I just don't want to deal with Ryan right now. He's been grumpy ever since we got back from Chicago, and I'm tired of listening to him complain."

"We'll see him at Christmas, though?"

"Don't remind me."

"I won't," Kelsey said, leaning up and giving Tyler a kiss.

"Are there any people you need to discuss?" he asked.

Kelsey thought. "I don't think so," she said. "My family is the same as always, although Dad's fussy about you. My friends are all too busy working to create any drama right now, and work is its usual level of crazy. My life is fine."

"What's with your mother and grandma?"

Kelsey shrugged. "Same as ever. It's not a issue. Let me ask you a question."

"OK."

"What happens if I start my own business?"

"What do you mean?" Tyler asked curiously.

"You're the CEO of a listed company, and I'm your wife. Do you think that's going to be a problem?"

"I doubt it. I guess it depends on what you want to do."

"I suppose so."

"I'm glad to see that you're thinking about how to become a billionaire," Tyler said.

"I might want to make partner first," Kelsey said.

"You won't make real money working for someone else," Tyler pointed out.

Kelsey knew this was probably true. There weren't enough hours in the day for an employee getting paid by the hour. As a lawyer who specialized in licensing, Kelsey was well aware of the power of having a product that wasn't tied to constant, consistent effort. Ryan had discussed this concept with Ben. There was a wide divide between creating a piece of software that you could sell billions of times, and getting up every morning to create a plate of food you could sell to one customer. It was the difference between Ben having to ask Tyler for money to invest, and Tyler having the money to give him.

"That's why I might want to make partner. If I come up with a good idea, I'll probably start my business first. It's a ways off, though. I'm happy with Simon," Kelsey sighed. "But I'm not going to make partner there."

"True. Bill Simon's not going to have any partners. If you want to make partner, you'll have to move to another firm."

Kelsey leaned her head against Tyler's arm. "I don't know why I'm thinking about this. I'm only in my second year."

"It's good to plan," Tyler replied.

"I guess," Kelsey said. "Should we go back? I'll teach you how to make cookies."

"Will I get kisses?" Tyler asked hopefully.

"All you want," Kelsey replied firmly.

"And we can go to Sequim later?" Tyler said suggestively.

"Absolutely," Kelsey said. She looked at her husband and her insides flip-flopped. She blushed and looked away and Tyler laughed.

"My bride is shy," he commented, kissing her again.

After a stop by the food co-op for supplies, Kelsey and Tyler walked back into the house. Grandma was sitting on the living room sofa, afghan in her lap. As Kelsey had predicted, Grandma Rose had done a lot of crocheting while they had been away.

"Wow, Grandma," Kelsey said, after they greeted her. "You've done a lot."

"It's very nice," Tyler added.

"Thank you. I hope when you take it back to Seattle, you'll remember me," Grandma said.

Kelsey felt a twinge of sadness. Every time she saw her, Kelsey was reminded of the fact that her grandmother was getting older. It was difficult for Kelsey.

"Of course we will," Kelsey said, as Tyler took the groceries into the kitchen. "You're unforgettable."

Grandma laughed.

"Do you want to join us in the kitchen? We're going to make cookies," Kelsey said, wiping the sadness from her mind. Her grandmother was here now, and that was a good thing.

"You two go ahead," Grandma said, continuing to crochet. Kelsey walked over and gave her grandmother a quick hug, then joined Tyler in the kitchen, where he had laid out their purchases.

"Are you ready?" Kelsey asked him.

"I think so. I do know how to cook," Tyler replied.

"Hmm," Kelsey said.

They washed their hands, then returned to the kitchen counter.

"What's first?" Tyler asked her expectantly.

"We need to heat the oven to 375 degrees," Kelsey said, turning it on. She pulled a beautiful white mixing bowl set with a green leaf pattern down from the cupboard. "Can you get the measuring cups and spoons?" she asked. Tyler opened a drawer and pulled both sets out. They were a bright shiny copper.

Kelsey opened the yellow box of baking soda that they had bought, then reached out for the flour and salt containers that were on the countertop.

"Please measure out two and a quarter cups of flour, a teaspoon of baking soda and a teaspoon of salt, and put them all in the big bowl," she said.

"What are you doing?" Tyler asked.

"Supervising," Kelsey teased, leaning against the counter.

"I thought we were making these together," Tyler said.

"We are. There's more to do," Kelsey said with a smile. She took the smaller of the two bowls and pulled it towards herself. She had left two sticks of butter out on the counter before they had gone on their walk and they were now soft. Kelsey unwrapped them and placed them in the bowl. To the butter bowl, she added 3/4 cup of white sugar, and a packed 3/4 cup of golden-brown sugar. Finally she added a teaspoon of the vanilla that she had found in the cupboard earlier in the day.

"Here," she said, holding the bottle out to him. "Have a sniff."

Tyler glanced at the label.

"It's Indian vanilla," Kelsey said. Tyler shrugged, and Kelsey looked at him curiously. "Margaret said you liked it," she added, seeing his look.

"Margaret would know," Tyler replied as Kelsey replaced the cap. She walked over to the refrigerator and pulled two eggs from a carton. As she returned to the counter, she realized that possibly Tyler didn't know his own preferences. Margaret, Jeffrey and a host of other people were paid to know Tyler's preferences for him.

"Can you add these to the butter, one at a time?" Kelsey asked. "No shell," she added.

"I knew that," Tyler said petulantly, as Kelsey giggled. Tyler carefully cracked the eggs and added their contents to the bowl. Once he was done, Kelsey picked up the bowl and gently mixed the combined flour mixture into the butter bowl. As she stirred the bowl, just until the contents were mixed, she said, "we need a cup and a half of chocolate chips, a half cup of the dried cranberries, and a half cup of the white chocolate chips."

"May I eat some?" Tyler asked, as he opened the gold bag of chocolate chips.

"Of course. Can I have a cranberry?" Kelsey asked him. Tyler obliged by putting one in her mouth. The sweetness of the added sugar contrasted with the tartness of the cranberry.

"Let's add a cup of nuts," Kelsey said, picking up another dried cranberry.

"No walnuts," Tyler commented to her. Kelsey knew that Tyler didn't like walnuts very much.

"I know, I bought pecans," Kelsey said, picking up the bag from the counter. "But either is fine."

"Not to me."

"So spoiled," Kelsey teased.

Tyler leaned over and kissed her on the lips. "Where do I put all these chips?" He asked.

"I'll mix them in," Kelsey said, lifting up the container that Tyler had put the chocolate chips in. "Can you measure one cup of pecans, please?"

"OK," Tyler said. Kelsey mixed the chocolate chips, cranberries, and white chocolate chips into the batter, mixing very slightly. She added the pecans that Tyler handed to her.

"You need this, right?" Tyler asked, handing her a melon baller as she stopped stirring the batter.

"How did you know that?" Kelsey asked.

"You used it when you and Ryan made cookies," Tyler said.

Kelsey thought back. "That was ages ago," she commented. "Our first summer of law school. You have a good memory."

"About you, I do," Tyler replied.

Kelsey blushed. She reached back into the cabinet and removed the non-stick baking sheets she had located earlier. She measured out teaspoon-sized balls of the cookie dough and dropped them onto the sheets.

"How long do we have to wait?" Tyler asked as he opened the oven and carefully placed the baking sheets inside.

"Nine minutes. Up to eleven. We just need to make sure that the edges are slightly golden," Kelsey said. She rinsed her hands in the sink, and as she did so, Tyler put his arms around her waist. He nuzzled her hair.

"I'm going to lose track of time," Kelsey fussed.

"Athena, set a timer for nine minutes," Tyler said.

"Nine minutes, starting now," the computerized voice of Athena replied.

"Problem solved," Tyler said, pulling Kelsey closer. She turned in his arms and looked up at him.

"You're trouble, Mr. Olsen," she said, kissing him.

"I'd like to get into trouble with you," Tyler replied. "When are we going to Sequim?"

"After dinner? I don't want Grandma asking too many questions," Kelsey replied.

"That's fine," Tyler said, kissing her neck. He ran his hands up her thighs. Kelsey felt herself getting warm.

"Grandma's in the next room," she protested as Tyler continued to kiss her.

"We're just kissing," Tyler said, pressing against her. Warm turned to hot for Kelsey.

Suddenly the doorbell rang. Tyler sighed.

"Again?" he said, breaking away from Kelsey.

"At least there's no one else that can move in," Kelsey said, smoothing down her hair. She knew she was flushed from Tyler's affection. They left the kitchen and walked out into the living room.

"Are you expecting anyone, Grandma?" Kelsey asked as the couple headed to the door.

"Not me, dear," Grandma said, as yarn flew through her fingers. Tyler opened the door, and to Kelsey's surprise, her parents stood on the doorstep.

"Come in," Tyler said, stepping aside for them.

"Hi, Mom," Dan North said, as he and Kelly North entered the living room.

Grandma looked up. She frowned, then looked back down at the afghan.

"Hi, honey," she replied, not looking at her son and his wife.

Tyler and Kelsey looked on, as Dan North glanced at his spouse.

"Rose, I'm very sorry. Please come back to our house," Kelly North said. Kelsey suspected that her mother spoke the words unwillingly.

"You don't mean it," Grandma Rose said, continuing to crochet.

"She does, Mom," Dan North said. "Come back home."

"I like it here," Grandma said.

"Kelsey and Tyler need some time alone," Kelly North said irritably.

"We're happy having Grandma here," Kelsey said.

"It's nice having Grandma around," Tyler added.

Kelsey smiled at him. Despite the fact that they had to sneak out of the house, Kelsey knew that Tyler meant it. He was as fond of Grandma as Kelsey was.

"All the same, we'd like you to come back, Mom," Dan North said. "We won't see you at Christmas, and it would be nice if we could have some time together too."

"So Kelly can call me senile again?" Grandma said.

"I didn't say that, Rose."

"You didn't say that in front of me. But I certainly heard it," Grandma retorted.

"Mom…"

"I don't want to go where I'm not welcome, Daniel," Grandma said firmly.

"Mom, you're always welcome in my house."

"It's not just your house," Grandma Rose pointed out.

Kelly North sighed. "Rose, you're always welcome in our house," she said. "Please come back."

Grandma Rose stopped crocheting and put the afghan to her side.

"I'd rather stay here," she said bluntly, looking at Kelly North, then Grandma picked up her crochet again.

Kelly North looked flustered, while Dan North gave a weary smile to his daughter. This wasn't new to Kelsey.

"Will the two of you excuse us?" Kelly North asked the young couple.

"We'll be in the kitchen," Kelsey said to Grandma, taking Tyler's hand and leading him out of the room. She knew why her mother had asked them to leave. Despite the fact that Tyler was her son-in-law now, Kelsey knew that Kelly North was mortified about having a family fight in front of him. The thought amused Kelsey. If her mother only knew what Tyler's family had fought about in front of Kelsey.

At the moment they stepped foot into the kitchen, the timer went off.

"Athena, stop," Tyler commanded, and the timer stopped instantly.

Kelsey peered inside the oven. "I think we're done," she said, grabbing a potholder. She pulled the baking trays out and set them down.

"They look good," Tyler said. "Now what do we do?"

"Let them sit on the baking sheet for three minutes, then we can place them on wire racks and let them cool completely," Kelsey said, opening a drawer and pulling out a spatula. She lifted a hot cookie off the baking sheet. "Or we can eat them," she said, pulling off a hot piece of cookie. The warm chocolate oozed all over her fingers as she popped the piece in her mouth.

"Delicious," she said.

Tyler took a piece of his own from the spatula and ate it.

"These are great, Kels," he said.

"Now you can bake them for us," Kelsey said brightly.

Tyler looked doubtful. "I think I'm still going to ask Margaret to do it," he commented.

"You can, but they won't be hot," Kelsey said, taking another bite of cookie.

"She can make the dough, and I can bake them," Tyler replied. "Three hundred and seventy-five degrees for nine minutes, right?"

"Right," Kelsey replied. They stood eating the warm cookies for a moment, then Dan North walked in.

"The crisis is over. Mom's coming home with us," he said.

"How did you pull that off?" Kelsey said, offering her father a cookie from the spatula. He took it.

"No idea. I'm going to tackle the Middle East peace talks next. I think they'll be easier," Kelsey's father said, popping the cookie into his mouth.

Kelsey put the spatula down. "Let's say goodbye to Grandma," she said to Tyler.

"Where were we?" Kelsey asked happily a short time later. Grandma Rose was safely back at her parents' house, and Tyler and Kelsey hadn't needed to pretend to go to Sequim. But a second after Kelsey asked the question, she involuntarily gasped in delight.

"Right there," her husband whispered into her ear, as he pulled her closer.

Kelsey glanced at her handsome husband that evening. He was holding her hand as they were walking in the cold drizzly rain on their way to the Jefferson house.

"Are you OK?" Kelsey asked him.

"Peachy," Tyler replied.

Kelsey giggled. "I'm sure things will be fine," she said soothingly. "What are you concerned about?"

"I just hope that I'm ready. Papa Jefferson's questions always throw me off balance."

"He's just concerned about me," Kelsey said.

"And Ben."

"Papa asked you questions about your investment in Ben's cafe to try to figure you out as a person. He's not concerned about Ben," Kelsey replied.

"Will I always have to prove myself to him, or will there come a point when he accepts that I'm your husband?" Tyler asked.

Kelsey thought he was sincere in his question. "Considering Papa's relationship with his actual son-in-law, I expect that he'll always have doubts about you too," she admitted.

"Great," Tyler said with sarcasm.

Kelsey squeezed Tyler's hand. "It doesn't matter. Dad thinks you're great, and we only see Papa a couple times a year."

"I'm not sure I agree with the first half of that sentence," Tyler commented.

"I'm Daddy's little girl, and you're the man who stole me away. But he knows that you're OK," Kelsey replied.

"I guess."

"We'll be visiting your mom next, and who knows how that will turn out," Kelsey commented, feeling a few butterflies in her stomach as she said it.

"It will turn out fine," Tyler said firmly. "Lisa knows how important you are to me, and she knows that she needs to get to know you better. Spending Christmas at her house is an opportunity for her to do so."

"Maybe," Kelsey said. She glanced at Tyler. "You're really worried about having dinner with Papa, aren't you?"

Tyler sighed.

Kelsey gave him a smile. "It will be fine," she said soothingly.

Fifteen minutes later, though, even Kelsey was having doubts. They had arrived on time, five minutes before their 6 p.m. meal. Jasmine and Jim had sent their apologies, as they were still in Brennan with Jim's family. Mama Jefferson had been pulling trays out of the oven as they had walked in, and she had shooed the couple out of the kitchen and into the living room where Papa had been waiting for them.

Tyler had made it through the pleasantries, during which he and Papa had discussed the Seahawks' chances for next season, and once they had sat at the dinner table, Tyler had breezed through a discussion of Ben's plans for the new restaurant. But the question that was currently on the table seemed to have Tyler stumped.

"Where do I see my career going?" Tyler repeated, utterly perplexed. Kelsey was confused as well.

"Papa, Tyler's going to be CEO of Tactec," Kelsey said. She had assumed that information was obvious to anyone who read about business, which Papa Jefferson certainly did.

"CEO is a title," Papa Jefferson patiently explained, as Mama Jefferson sat at the table, eating the Greek lasagna in front of her. "I want to know what you're actually going to do."

Tyler bit his lip. Kelsey knew that he was trying to formulate an answer for Papa, who seemed intensely curious about Tyler's response.

"I'm not sure," Tyler admitted. Kelsey knew it was exactly the wrong thing to say.

"You've been working for Tactec for six months, and you don't know?" Papa pressed.

"I'm not CEO yet."

"Obviously, but you must have learned something about the company in six months," Papa commented.

"I have," Tyler replied.

"What have you learned?"

"That it's run at the whims of its two founders," Tyler replied.

"So what will you do differently as CEO?"

"Run it as an actual company," Tyler replied.

"That's a start. What does that mean?" Papa asked.

"I'm not sure what you're asking me," Tyler admitted.

Papa pondered Tyler for a moment. Kelsey thought she knew what the look meant. Papa was trying to decide whether Tyler was being stubborn, or if he actually didn't understand the question. Papa Jefferson took a bite of his food, then began again.

"How do you feel about Kelsey's Instagram page?" Papa Jefferson asked. If he had been anyone else, Kelsey would have thought the question was random, but being that it was from Papa, she knew that it wasn't. Papa was trying to lead Tyler to a point, but she had no idea what that point was.

"Feel?" Tyler asked.

Papa Jefferson frowned, just a little bit. "Kelsey's Instagram page has millions of followers, and the company that you work for runs it as if it were a corporate asset, with product placements and press releases."

Kelsey had to admit that this was true. Along with posts featuring Daisy's new insights about Kelsey, the Kelsey Olsen Instagram page had been teasing several new Tactec products that would be released just in time for Christmas.

Papa continued. "So based on what you're saying about the company, the reason that Kelsey's popularity is being exploited for corporate gain is because founders want it that way."

"Papa," Kelsey cut in, "It's a family business, and it's not really my Instagram page. I don't mind."

"I'm sure that you don't, Kelsey, but I'd like to hear what Tyler has to say about it."

Tyler looked at Papa Jefferson thoughtfully. From his look, Kelsey realized that Tyler was starting to understand what Papa was getting at. Kelsey was still in the dark, though.

"Are you asking me how I would run Tactec differently? Using Kelsey's Instagram as an example?"

"Sure, let's start there," Papa said to him.

"I'd pay her," Tyler shrugged.

"Why don't you?" Papa asked.

Kelsey opened her mouth to speak, but then closed it. She knew that Papa wouldn't want her to interrupt Tyler's answer.

"I'm not the CEO," Tyler replied. Kelsey could tell that Papa didn't like that answer, but before he could speak, Tyler continued. "But beginning next month, Kelsey will be paid, retroactive to June."

Kelsey looked at Tyler in surprise. This was the first that she had heard about Instagram payments.

"Why?" she blurted out.

"You're a celebrity," Tyler said to Kelsey. "You have millions of followers, and a really high engagement level. There's no reason why Tactec should be able to promote itself for free using your name."

Papa looked pleased, but Kelsey felt troubled. As Kelsey Olsen, she was famous, but of course it was due to her relationship with Tyler.

"What will Kelsey be paid?" Papa asked Tyler.

"Market rate. Tactec has other deals with Instagrammers, so Kelsey will receive a similar rate, based on her influence."

"Tyler, I'm your wife," Kelsey protested. "How will it look for me to get paid for promoting Tactec on my Instagram page?"

"You'll be paid directly by the CEO," Tyler replied. Kelsey frowned at his words, but she took one look into his chocolate-brown eyes, and saw the determination there. There was no use in complaining. Tyler would insist that she take the money.

"Good," Papa Jefferson said, in a pleased tone. "I'm glad to see that you don't think exploiting your wife is good business."

"I'm not being exploited," Kelsey said grumpily.

"When I become CEO," Tyler said, "I want there to be a stronger division between my family and the company. I think it will be better for both parties."

"What else will be different?" Papa asked.

"I'll probably make more decisions based on research, instead of instinct."

"Well, you don't have the instincts of someone who created a billion-dollar company, so I imagine that's a good idea," Papa said.

Tyler ignored the comment, although Kelsey didn't think it was particularly nice.

"I guess I would like Tactec to be a little more focused on finances and less on placing bets on untested ideas."

"But won't you lose Tactec's innovation edge?" Papa asked.

"That's a possibility," Tyler replied, "But if we paid slightly more attention to our bottom line, and wasted less money on bad ideas, we wouldn't need to have so many wins. It's a trade-off, but I want the company to succeed in the long run."

"Second-guessing the current CEO?" Papa Jefferson asked.

"You did ask me what I would do differently," Tyler pointed out.

"Fair enough," Papa replied. "So Tactec is going to become more boring with you as CEO?"

To Kelsey's surprise, Tyler laughed.

"Wall Street likes boredom. Profits quarter after quarter," Tyler said.

"But what about your customers? What happens if you aren't delivering new and exciting goods year after year?"

"I think we still will," Tyler said. "I'm not against investing in ideas. I just want to be smarter about it."

"Interesting," Papa said, and from his tone, Kelsey could tell that Papa Jefferson was satisfied by Tyler's answer. Kelsey turned to Tyler and gave him a wink. She thought she saw a look of relief in Tyler's eyes as Papa turned back to his food. Once again, Tyler had survived dinner with Papa Jefferson.

A few hours later, Kelsey lay in bed with Tyler, his arms wrapped around her warm body. He nuzzled her cheek.

"I'm sorry it's such a trial to be with me," Kelsey said, leaning against him, her eyes closed.

"What do you mean?"

"Dad. Papa. Oh, and Mom and Grandma of course."

"Don't be silly, I love you. They just come along with you."

"Like a tick," Kelsey said.

Tyler laughed. "They're family. Not clingy insects," he commented.

"Some days it's hard to tell," Kelsey teased.

"No it isn't."

"You did good with Papa."

"Thanks. I had no idea what he was talking about at first."

"I don't need any money," Kelsey said.

"Papa has a point. It's not fair to you. In a few weeks, Jeffrey will be dropping off the Tactec holiday line, and trying to convince you to walk around town carrying a new phone or tablet. You don't get paid when the paparazzi take pictures of you, so this is the least Tactec should do."

"Yeah, but it's not Tactec. It's Lisa," Kelsey pointed out.

"It would be too hard to justify payments to my new wife to the board. It's just easier if Lisa pays you."

"It's weird."

"It's fine. As CEO, Lisa has flexperks that she never uses. She'll pay you out of that."

"Flexperks?" Kelsey asked. She had never heard the term.

"It's discretionary cash. Like an allowance," Tyler replied.

"An allowance?" Kelsey asked, amused. "I thought Lisa didn't take a salary."

"She doesn't, but she keeps everything else. Her car, driver, security. Everything that comes with the CEO title."

"So I'll be paid out of petty cash?"

"Exactly."

"I won't quit my day job then," Kelsey teased.

"I think you probably could," Tyler replied. "Then you could stay in bed with me," he added.

"Very tempting, Mr. Olsen," Kelsey said, putting her hand on his chest, and cuddling against him. "I'll give it some thought."

"If only," Tyler replied.

"I'm here now," Kelsey said, opening her eyes and looking at him.

Tyler gave her a broad smile.

"That you are," he replied, kissing her.

After a surprisingly pleasant brunch with the North family on Sunday — and a couple more blissful hours in their bedroom — Kelsey and Tyler drove to Kingston, and to the ferry that would take them back to their side of Puget Sound.

"Did you have a nice time, Princess?" Tyler asked, reaching out his finger to wipe whipped cream off Kelsey's nose. They were sitting in the car, watching as the ferry they were about to board docked.

"Port Townsend was great," Kelsey said, taking another bite of the warm crepe they had purchased while waiting.

"I'm sort of surprised to hear you say that," Tyler commented.

"You were in the hot seat, not me. It was a nice change."

Tyler laughed. "You have a point."

"You didn't have fun?"

"I had fun with you," Tyler said, leaning over and kissing Kelsey's neck. She felt herself blush.

"We're waiting for the ferry, Tyler."

"And what will we be doing on the ferry, Mrs. Olsen?" Tyler asked her seductively.

"Sitting in the car, and waiting for the ferry to dock in Edmonds," Kelsey replied.

"So I should think of things to do with you in the car?"

"We'll be sitting," Kelsey repeated.

"We could be doing something else," Kelsey noted the look in Tyler's eyes, and she felt a tingle up her spine.

"No, we won't be doing anything else," she said, a little more doubtfully than she wanted to.

"Are you sure?"

"Positive."

"I don't think so," Tyler said, leaning over and kissing her once more.

"Why are you always trying to get me into trouble?" Kelsey groused.

"I'm not trying to get you into trouble. I'm trying to get you into bed."

"We just got out of bed," Kelsey pointed out.

"That was over an hour ago," Tyler said.

"There's no bed in the car," Kelsey said.

"We can improvise," Tyler replied. He flipped a switch, and Kelsey felt her seat gently begin to recline. "See, a bed," Tyler said.

Kelsey reached her hand out and flipped the switch to put the seat back in its upright position. She glared at Tyler.

"The bed's back in Seattle. You can wait."

Tyler shook his head. "I don't want to."

"You will," Kelsey replied firmly. "Finish your crepe," she ordered, taking a bite of her own.

"Am I testing your willpower, Mrs. Olsen?"

"You always are, Mr Olsen," Kelsey replied, but she smiled.

When she was back in the office on Monday, Kelsey felt happy and refreshed, and she knew that the long weekend had done her some good. She also felt some relief. Not only had Margaret saved Thanksgiving dinner, but Kelsey had also managed to get through another visit to Port Townsend and her family.

Kelsey always had mixed emotions about returning to Port Townsend. Invariably she could expect some drama, and almost always, Kelsey's mother was involved, just as she had been on this visit.

Kelsey jumped right back into her cases when she got to her desk, because she knew that there was a lot of work to be done before Bill Simon closed the office for the holidays and the last two weeks of the year.

Kelsey sat at her desk, typing furiously away, a half-eaten salad at her side on Tuesday afternoon. She paused, took a quick glance at her work, and made a couple more changes. Then she took her hands off the keyboard, picked up her fork, and ate a bite of salad. Bill wanted this project done today, even though it hadn't been promised to the client until Friday. Kelsey was a little nervous about why. She suspected that Bill had another project waiting for her that he had yet to mention.

After a few more bites of salad, Kelsey returned to her work. But within seconds, someone walked up to her door. Kelsey looked up in surprise.

"Hello, Kelsey," Lisa Olsen said to her.

"Hi, Lisa," Kelsey said. "Come in," she added, as Lisa was still standing in the doorway.

"Thank you," Lisa said as she glided into the office. "May I?" she asked, gesturing to the client chair.

"Of course," Kelsey said, in confusion. *What was Lisa doing here?*

"I'm waiting for Bill," Lisa said, in answer to the unspoken question. "He's on the phone."

Kelsey felt relief, and chastised herself for it. Lisa had been nothing but gracious after their rocky start, and Kelsey had been trying and failing to accept Lisa's new kindness. It bothered Kelsey that she hadn't been able to get beyond the emotions of the past, particularly since she knew that Tyler wanted her to do so. Kelsey resolved to work on it during the Christmas holiday, when they would be at Lisa's house. But of course, she had a small opportunity to be pleasant now.

"How are you?" Kelsey asked politely. "Did you have a nice Thanksgiving?"

Lisa looked thoughtful for a moment, then she replied.

"It was fine. I'm looking forward to you and Tyler being at home for Christmas. Does your family have any special traditions that we should celebrate?"

Kelsey smiled. The only real tradition that the North family had was Kelsey playing the Christmas elf and handing out presents.

"No," Kelsey said. "I'm looking forward to seeing what traditions Tyler grew up with," she added, but it wasn't completely true. According to Tyler, there was a lot of reviewing of fourth-quarter spreadsheets during Christmas with the Olsens.

"I'm sure that we'll have a nice time," Lisa replied pleasantly.

"Lisa," Bill Simon said from Kelsey's doorway. Kelsey thought Bill looked a little flushed, as if he had hurried across the office.

Lisa coolly looked over her shoulder at him.

"Are you avoiding me, Bill?" Lisa asked bluntly.

Bill Simon frowned. "Kelsey, can you give us a minute?" he said.

Kelsey was caught by surprise, but she stood up instantly.

"Of course," Kelsey said, and she left her office. Bill closed the door behind her.

"What's going on?" Millie asked. She, Amie and Tori were all standing a few feet away from Kelsey's office, and it was clear that they had followed Bill, who was now inside Kelsey's office, talking to Lisa.

"No idea," Kelsey said. She and the others looked into the glass walls of Kelsey's office. Kelsey thought that at this moment, Bill, like Tyler, would have appreciated curtains for the glass walls. Lisa remained in her chair, but her body language had shifted. She was clearly displeased.

The four women watched as the conversation went on. It was impossible to hear, yet it was evident that emotions were running high in the room. Kelsey considered her answer to Millie's question, and realized that she did have an idea about what was going on. Lisa wanted to know if Bill had been avoiding her.

Kelsey thought about the past few weeks. She hadn't seen Bill and Lisa together since Chicago. Kelsey knew that Lisa had been attending events alone and that Bill had gone to Arizona with Bob Perkins for Thanksgiving. And of course Margaret had said that he hadn't been at the estate. Bill had been avoiding Lisa, just as Lisa had said.

And as she stood, awkwardly — but still curiously — watching the heated discussion in her own office, Kelsey realized that she, unlike the people she was standing with, knew exactly why.

She thought back to her conversation with Bill about people drinking around him. Bill had felt that those who had complained about his drinking shouldn't drink around him. Kelsey knew that Lisa and Bill's relationship had fallen apart decades ago because of Bill's drinking. Yet Lisa had become drunk in Chicago — so much so, that she had needed to sleep it off. It all made sense.

As she watched them, Kelsey felt some unease. She knew that Tyler would be perfectly happy for his mother to end her relationship with Kelsey's boss. But Kelsey had seen what kind of couple Bill and Lisa were. It was clear to her that they were in love. And despite her husband's feelings, Kelsey couldn't help but want them to work things out.

The discussion continued, but despite her awkwardness, Kelsey continued to stand. Unlike everyone else, she really didn't have another place to go. Bill and Lisa had chosen her office for their conversation, and it had happened so fast, Kelsey hadn't had time to even grab her computer. So she stood next to Millie, her office slippers on her feet.

Although she couldn't hear any words, Kelsey sensed that there had been a shift in the conversation. Lisa had uncrossed her arms, and relaxed in the chair, while Bill was leaning against Kelsey's desk, instead of the unyielding military stance he had been in moments earlier.

After what seemed a long time, Lisa Olsen stood up. As she did so, she spotted the women outside the glass. She said something to Bill, and he laughed. Lisa stood up and tossed her long dark hair over her shoulder. Bill began to walk toward the door, and Kelsey watched as her three co-workers scattered. They all ended up at the copier, which suddenly held fascination for them.

Bill opened the door of Kelsey's office, and he and Lisa left the room.

"Thanks, Kelsey," Bill said to her. Kelsey gave him a nod, and she couldn't help but smile as she saw Bill take Lisa's hand.

"I'll walk you out," Bill said to Lisa.

"Goodbye, Kelsey. I'll see you soon," Lisa said to her.

"Bye, Lisa," Kelsey replied as they walked away.

As Kelsey knew would be true, Tyler was less pleased that his mother and her boyfriend had worked out their differences. There was an unhappy look on her husband's face as she straightened his tie on Saturday night. They were heading to a holiday charity event at the Fairmont, and Margaret had informed Tyler that Bill would be in attendance.

"I thought he was gone," Tyler mused.

"Did you really?" Kelsey asked.

"Hope springs eternal," Tyler replied.

"Why don't you like him?" Kelsey asked, giving Tyler a kiss on the lips. "Really?"

Tyler looked thoughtful, and Kelsey wondered if he had an answer. There were a dozen potential reasons why Tyler objected. The fact that Tyler's relationship with Bill Simon had always been contentious, that Lisa had broken up with Bill once before — even the fact that Bill was a recovering alcoholic, Kelsey noted, were all possibilities.

Tyler sighed deeply. "I don't know," he finally said.

"You don't know?" Kelsey asked in surprise. She believed Tyler was sincere, but she was puzzled.

"No," Tyler replied.

"You must know why," Kelsey pressed. "Do you think he's not good enough for her?"

"I know he's not."

"Is it because you don't get along with him?" Kelsey asked.

"I don't want to talk about this," Tyler said. "I have to see him in fifteen minutes."

"Don't you think that you need to work this out?" Kelsey asked him, undaunted. Tyler had strong feelings about his mother's relationship, but as far as Kelsey was concerned, he had never worked through them.

"Why now?" Tyler asked.

"Because you told Zach that Bill is going to propose to Lisa in the next month. So I know that you've been thinking about it, even though you haven't been talking about it," Kelsey replied. "And we only have two weekends before the long holiday, when Bill's probably going to be around. So now seems like a good time."

"Maybe I'm wrong. Maybe he won't propose."

"Suppose you're right?"

"Suppose I am? Lisa says yes, and I deal with my feelings," Tyler replied.

"But the question is how will you deal with your feelings?" Kelsey said, and she felt the worry in her words.

"What do you mean?" Tyler asked curiously.

Kelsey frowned. "I'm worried about you," she admitted. "Between dealing with Chris and my family, I feel like you haven't had a lot of time to process what you think about Lisa and Bill."

"There hasn't been a lot to process," Tyler said. "They haven't seen each other in a month."

"There's something to process now," Kelsey pointed out.

"I really don't want to talk about this," Tyler said, with some finality.

Kelsey surveyed him. Tyler looked back at her, conceding nothing.

"Fine," Kelsey said. "I'll let it go for now. But I really think that you need to work through this."

"I'll give it some thought, Kelsey," Tyler said. Kelsey took his hand and they left the room.

As they sat together at their table a half hour later, Kelsey suspected that her words had had an impact on Tyler, even though he hadn't mentioned the topic of Lisa and Bill again.

"I think you should stay out of it." Lisa was saying to Bob, her long hair gleaming in the candlelight. Bill had left the table to get a drink for his date.

"That's because he's not your son," Bob replied.

"There's nothing wrong with not eating meat, Bob," Lisa said.

"It's weird. It's not like we can't afford it."

Lisa narrowed her eyes at him. "I think that you are taking your Midwestern heritage too far."

"Come on, you think it's weird too," Bob replied.

Lisa laughed. "Of course I do, but Ryan's weird. Anyway, it's perfectly healthy. Maybe healthier."

"You don't really believe that."

"Bob, you don't need to eat meat," Lisa said dismissively.

"Speak for yourself," Bob replied, taking a drink of his whiskey.

Lisa laughed again as Bill returned with drinks in hand. "Thank you," she said to Bill, her eyes sparkling at her boyfriend as she took her drink.

"My pleasure," Bill said, sitting next to her.

Kelsey glanced at her husband, who was frowning as he read an article on his phone.

"Where's your date?" Bill asked Bob.

Kelsey wasn't surprised that Bob looked at her before he spoke. She knew that until Bob and Morgan had truly ended their relationship, Kelsey would continue to find herself in the middle of it.

"Arizona. She missed her flight."

"You didn't send a plane down for her?" Bill asked.

"She said that I didn't need to," Bob shrugged.

"Fiona's very independent," Bill commented.

"That's not the word I would use," Lisa said.

"And what word would you use?" Bob asked in amusement.

"Stubborn," Lisa replied.

"You would know, missy," Bob said, teasing her.

"No, Lisa's right. Fiona's a handful," Bill said.

"I love how the two of you are experts after spending a total of three hours with her over the past year," Bob said.

"It takes six seconds to size someone up," Tyler piped in, without looking up from his phone.

"Quiet. You haven't met her."

"I haven't been invited to," Tyler replied.

"Do you want to?" Bob asked.

"Not really," Tyler replied.

Lisa laughed. "Good call," she said.

Bob frowned. "You don't like her?" he asked Lisa.

"I'm not sure she's the right woman for you," Lisa demurred. "But as long as you aren't serious about her, she's fine."

"Bob's not serious about anyone, so it's OK," Bill said.

"Why do I talk to you two?" Bob asked, taking another sip of whiskey.

The conversation about Fiona over, the trio moved on to new topics, while Tyler continued to look at his phone and Kelsey considered the dynamics of the group as the program began. After spending a weekend with her actual family, it was a little strange to be with them.

As it was, in all the time Kelsey had known Tyler, she had only spent significant time with two of his family members — Tyler's mother and father. Yet in Tyler's life, there were many people who were virtual family members, although they were not related by blood. Bob, Chris's ex-girlfriend Liz, even Ryan all counted in this group.

It was part of the reason that Kelsey felt that Tyler needed to determine how he felt about Bill Simon — because from Kelsey's perceptive, over the past few months, Bill had joined Tyler's family too.

"You survived," Kelsey teased as she and Tyler left the ballroom.

"It was touch and go for a while," Tyler admitted. "But now I can pay attention to you instead of my phone."

"What were you reading about?"

"How to break up a relationship."

"You were not," Kelsey replied with a frown.

"I was. There were some very interesting tips on the internet," Tyler said with a smile.

"Tips that you aren't going to follow."

"Whose side are you on?"

"The right side," Kelsey said.

"I don't think so," Tyler said.

"If you don't know why you don't like him, then you shouldn't be plotting to break them up."

"That's your opinion."

"It is. And I'm right."

Tyler kissed her hand. "I'll think about it," he said.

Kelsey glanced at him, then her eyes turned to the sparkling lights around them. As always, the Fairmont was dressed up for the holidays.

"Should we go see the trees?" Tyler asked her.

"We should," Kelsey beamed.

As they walked around the lower lobby of the hotel, stopping at trees, Kelsey couldn't help but be curious about whether Tyler had bought one for her. They had seen the one that Ryan had ordered for Jessica and the babies, which was pink, blue, and covered in handmade ornaments commemorating the twins' birth — but despite the fact that Kelsey and Tyler had celebrated a milestone of their own this year, she hadn't seen a tree for her.

"I think that's it," Tyler said, as they reached the last tree in the lobby. As they did every year, Tactec had also ordered a tree to benefit charity, and just like every other year, the ornaments were a bright Tactec red.

"They were beautiful," Kelsey said, hiding her disappointment. She hated to admit it, but this year, she was really hoping for a tree with memories of their wedding.

"I guess Jessica will see hers next week," Tyler said.

"I won't spoil the surprise," Kelsey replied as the doorman opened the front door of the Fairmont, and they walked out into the cool evening.

"Are you warm enough?" Tyler asked. "We can take a taxi home."

"It's fine."

"How about your shoes?"

Kelsey looked down at her feet. She was wearing sparkles of her own, cream-colored heels, decked out in rhinestones.

"I think I'll be OK. We'll walk slowly," she said, holding Tyler's arm and giving him a smile.

Fifteen minutes later, Tyler was kissing Kelsey in the elevator as they rode up to their home. Kelsey looked into Tyler's sexy brown eyes, as he caressed her.

"I'm glad we're home," Kelsey whispered as Tyler kissed her.

"Why? Do you have plans for me?" Tyler asked, as he kissed his way down her chest. The elevator stopped and the doors opened.

"I…" Kelsey said, but she paused. Their home was completely dark. "Did the lights go out?" she asked.

Tyler turned toward the open elevator door.

"Let's find out," he said. He took Kelsey's hand and led her out of the elevator. But instead of stopping to take off their shoes, Tyler led Kelsey a few additional steps forward, and Kelsey shouted with happiness.

"Thank you, Tyler!" she said, throwing her arms around him in glee. In the living room, a beautiful Christmas tree sparkled in the darkness. Kelsey released Tyler, kicked off her heels and carefully ran through the darkened room toward it. "Wow," she said in awe.

The tree was amazing. In the twinkling light were photos of their wedding, hand-crafted ornaments made from the lace of Kelsey's grandmother's wedding gown, and tiny wedding bouquets that resembled Kelsey's own. Kelsey felt tears come to her eyes, and she turned and gave Tyler a hug.

"It's beautiful. Thank you," she said.

"You're welcome, Princess," Tyler said.

Kelsey turned back to the tree, Tyler's arms around her waist, as she looked at it once more. But this time, she noticed something else sparkle from the branches. She reached out, and pulled a diamond bracelet from the branches.

"Tyler," Kelsey whispered, as she looked at it. It was stunning — three rows of diamonds woven into an elegant design.

"Happy December," he replied, kissing her once more.

"Do you really think we're going to get our two-week vacation this year?" Jake asked Kelsey on Monday. He was in her office, and they were going over the current IP cases. There were a ton.

"I think so," Kelsey said optimistically, but she also had her doubts.

"That didn't sound convincing," Jake pointed out.

"I'm doing what I can," Kelsey replied.

Jake laughed. "We need some help," he commented.

"We're not going to get any."

"That I know," Jake agreed.

Kelsey sighed. "I think we need a plan."

"Quit?" Jake said brightly.

"That wasn't what I was thinking," Kelsey replied. "Actually, I'm not sure that it matters. Bill's just going to come to me if there's an emergency, because I'll be around. It's not like I can hide from him, I'm staying at Lisa's house."

"That's unbelievable."

"What?"

"'I'm staying at Lisa Olsen's house.' You're so casual about spending your vacation at the estate of the CEO of Tactec," Jake pointed out.

"She's my mother-in-law, Jake," Kelsey said, but she knew that he was right. A lot of things had become normal to her over the past few months that weren't really normal at all.

"I guess I won't feel guilty about you doing all the work then. Between getting yelled at by Bill, you can hang out in the sauna, or have your chef make you fancy desserts," Jake commented.

Kelsey didn't know what to say, because it was completely true.

"Just enjoy your vacation," Kelsey said to him. Jake gave her a grin.

"It's cozy," Tyler said, nuzzling her hair that night.

"Very," Kelsey replied happily. They were cuddled under the afghan that Grandma Rose had crocheted for them, a fire blazing in the glass fireplace across from them.

Tyler hugged her more tightly and Kelsey snuggled against his chest. It felt so good to be held by him.

"I love you so much," he said to her.

"I love you too."

"I have something I need to tell you."

"What's that?" Kelsey asked him.

"I need to go back to New York," Tyler said.

Kelsey looked up at him in surprise. "For how long?"

"Three days? Hopefully not longer."

"Is Chris OK?" Kelsey asked in concern.

"Yeah, but I need to check on him. I hate leaving you, though."

"I can go with you."

"If you go now, Bill's going to try to take it out of your vacation," Tyler replied.

Kelsey was silent, because she knew that Tyler was probably right. It was one thing working on an as-needed basis at home during the holiday, but it was another thing being stuck in the office. Three days was a lot of time at Simon and Associates, and Kelsey knew that Bill wouldn't give it away without a fight — because unlike before, Kelsey's presence in New York wasn't needed.

"Maybe. When will you leave?"

"Tuesday. I'll be back for the weekend."

Kelsey nodded unhappily. "Why do you have to go?" she asked.

"Chris wants to leave the rehabilitation center, but Liz and the doctors don't think he's ready to go. In the meantime, Felipe is panicking, because Chris is pushing him to throw a holiday party at the gallery, but Felipe doesn't think he's ready to throw a big party yet. If I go to New York, I can deal with everything at once."

"I wish you could send Jeffrey."

"He's there now. That's why I know that I need to go. Jeffrey tried and failed to solve all of the problems that have cropped up since we left."

"I'm going to miss you," Kelsey said sadly.

"I'll miss you too, Princess. I'll hurry back," Tyler said, holding her. Kelsey stroked his chest, and leaned her head back on him.

Kelsey had trouble sleeping on Tuesday night. At 5 a.m. on Wednesday, Kelsey gave up trying to sleep and headed for the in-home gym to run. She felt unsettled with Tyler away.

Kelsey finished her exercise, got dressed and ate a leisurely breakfast, since she was up so early. Fifteen minutes before she usually left home, she headed out the door.

As Kelsey headed towards First Avenue, she was startled by someone approaching her.

"Hey, girly, give me some money," the man said to her. Kelsey glanced at the man, one of downtown Seattle's homeless, and continued to walk.

"I don't have anything," she said quietly, looking away.

"Look at the way you're dressed," the man said disparagingly, "Those shoes cost more than some people's rent."

"Beat it," Kelsey heard another voice say. She breathed a sigh of relief. It was Conor.

"We're just talking," the man said.

"Talk to someone else, or you'll be talking to me," Conor replied menacingly. "Make sure I don't see you again," he added. At Conor's words, the man wandered off.

"Thanks," Kelsey said, as Conor walked next to her. He was wearing a gray sweatshirt, sweatpants, and running shoes. "Were you out running?"

"No," Conor replied.

Kelsey was puzzled. "Then how did you see me?" she asked. Every morning Kelsey walked up to Simon's office alone. Jade had told Kelsey that she didn't need a bodyguard on her walk to work.

"We shadow you every morning, Kelsey."

"You do?" Kelsey said in surprise. She had never noticed Jade or Conor on her morning walks.

"Today was my day, but you left earlier than usual, so I didn't have time to dress up," Conor said.

"I had no idea you were following me," Kelsey said. "Why didn't you tell me?"

"We didn't want you to feel like you had lost your independence," Conor replied.

"I don't mind. I appreciate the two of you looking out for me. Especially today," she added.

"It's part of the job," Conor said with a smile.

Once Kelsey was settled into her office, she considered what had happened. She didn't mind at all that Conor and Jade had been following her without her knowledge. In fact, there was a part of her that had expected it.

What did trouble Kelsey was her comment to the homeless man. It had been unthinking, words that many people said when approached for money on the street. This time, though, Kelsey had been challenged, because even to the stranger on the street, it was clear that Kelsey's declaration wasn't true.

She didn't intend to start handing money out on the street, but she knew that it was time to start working on something that kept getting put aside. It was time to work on the Kelsey and Tyler Olsen Foundation.

"Tyler!" Kelsey shouted on Friday afternoon.

"Hey," Tyler replied, dropping a duffel bag in the client chair, then scooping Kelsey into his arms. She covered him in kisses, and he replied with kisses for her.

"I missed you," she said, hugging him tightly.

"I missed you too," Tyler said, holding her close.

"The party's all set?" Kelsey asked. She had spoken to Tyler every night he had been in New York, but as of yesterday evening, he was still working with the team at the gallery on the details for the holiday party."

"I certainly hope so," Tyler said.

"You're not going back," Kelsey asked.

"No. Jeffrey will attend on my behalf."

"How does Chris feel about that?"

"I don't care," Tyler replied. "Chris isn't paying me to host parties at the gallery. Or at all."

"Are you tired?"

"A little," Tyler admitted.

Kelsey gave Tyler a hug. Bob Perkins had joined Tyler on the trip to New York — and in addition to working for Chris, Tyler had also been working for Tactec.

"Did you have any fun at all?" she asked.

"I saw Liz, but she was angry at Chris, so it wasn't a great time."

"I'm glad that you're home. We'll have fun here," Kelsey said.

"OK. Jade's been walking you to work?"

"Yes," Kelsey said. She assumed that Conor had told Tyler about her encounter on Wednesday morning.

"All right," Tyler said, holding her. "When can you come home?"

"Midnight?"

Tyler sighed. "Earlier?" he asked.

"I'll try."

"I'll make it worth your while," Tyler said, kissing her.

Kelsey suddenly felt warm. "I thought you were tired," she teased.

"I'm never too tired for you," Tyler replied, kissing her again.

On Saturday, Kelsey sat in her office working as Tyler made notes on his Tactec tablet.

"I should just have Jeffrey do this tomorrow," Tyler said.

"You only have one Christmas gift to pick out," Kelsey said, looking up with a smile.

"I never know what to buy for Lisa, but if I tell Jeffrey to do it, he'll tell her that he did. This is why I don't go to Medina."

"What was the last gift you bought for her?"

Tyler was thoughtful. "It's been a while. Usually, we just go out for dinner."

"She's your mother, she'll like anything that you get for her."

"That's probably true."

"It's not like she's going to return it," Kelsey added.

Tyler laughed. "No, I guess not," he said.

"Can you ask Camille?" Kelsey knew that Camille, Lisa Olsen's assistant, probably knew everything about her.

"I asked Camille. She said that Lisa hasn't requested anything lately. Camille hasn't bought anything for Lisa in months."

"Nothing?"

"Nothing except event clothes."

"That's a problem," Kelsey said. "You could buy her a book."

"I'll search 'gifts for billionaires'," Tyler said, typing into his tablet.

"Do you seriously think something will come up?" Kelsey scoffed.

"A crystal-studded water bottle," Tyler said, reading off the list. "A gold-plated coffee maker."

Kelsey laughed. "I don't think so," she said.

"A tank? That could come in handy the next time she has to deal with Rick Burton," Tyler mused.

"Where would you put that?"

"Backyard?" Tyler shrugged.

"A million-dollar lawn ornament," Kelsey commented.

"I wonder what Bill is getting for her," Tyler mused. "I really hope it's not a ring."

"Don't think about it. It will stress you out more," Kelsey said.

"True."

"Did you think about why you don't like him?" Kelsey asked.

"No," Tyler replied. Kelsey looked at him, and Tyler read her look. "I'll think about it this weekend," he added.

"You might want to, since he's going to be at the Tactec party next weekend," Kelsey replied.

"No he won't," Tyler said.

"What do you mean?"

"Lisa never takes anyone to the Tactec party," Tyler replied.

"Why not?"

"They might overshadow her and Bob. She doesn't want anyone to be distracted by paying attention to who she's dating."

Kelsey thought Lisa had a point. The holiday party was supposed to be a work function.

"Bob sometimes has a date," Kelsey said.

"No one cares who Bob is dating," Tyler replied.

Kelsey considered Tyler's words. There were two ways to think about them. One way to think about it was that Bob dated so many people that it wasn't interesting to employees, but the other way was a lot less flattering. Perhaps people felt that as a man, Bob's dates wouldn't have an influence over the company, but Lisa's dates might.

She pushed the thought aside. Kelsey didn't like the thought that there were those who considered her simply arm candy for Tyler, although Kelsey knew that there were at least some people who did.

"I see," Kelsey replied.

Tyler surveyed her. "Are you nervous?" he asked.

Kelsey looked at him startled. "About what?"

"About being on display next weekend."

"What do you mean?"

"You realize that we aren't going to be able to just sit at the table and eat dessert with Zach this year. Everyone wants to meet you."

"Everyone who?"

"The executive team, my co-workers. Everyone wants to meet Kelsey Olsen."

"I don't think so."

"You have no idea," Tyler replied, and Kelsey saw that he was serious.

"Really?" she said. She hadn't been nervous before, but now she was feeling a bit of pressure.

"Sorry," Tyler said.

"It's fine. It's one night," Kelsey said, casually. But once again her stomach had butterflies.

"So I'm feeling a little guilty," Kelsey said as her makeup artist brushed highlighter on her cheeks.

"Why?" Jessica asked. She was sitting next to Kelsey in a chair, having makeup put on as well. They were in Jessica's house, getting ready for the Tactec party.

"I really wanted a Christmas tree." Kelsey replied as her makeup artist turned away to get eyeshadow from her kit.

"So? Didn't Tyler buy you one?"

"Yes. He did."

"So what is there to feel guilty about?" Jessica asked, stepping down from her own chair. Her makeup artist was done. Jessica looked at Kelsey, a halo of auburn curls framing her face.

"I don't know. I guess I feel a little selfish. I mean Tyler buys so much for me already. I really didn't need a tree."

"We don't need anything that the boys buy for us," Jessica said. "But there's nothing wrong with wanting something for yourself occasionally. Anyway, it was for charity."

"I guess."

Jessica pondered Kelsey silently as the makeup artist put finishing touches on Kelsey's makeup.

"You're all set, Mrs. Olsen," the makeup artist finally said.

"Thank you," Kelsey replied with a smile.

"I'll escort you out," Jade said to the makeup artist as Kelsey carefully stood up from the chair. Jessica's makeup artist had already left to go to Lisa Olsen's house and do her makeup.

Jessica watched them leave, then turned to Kelsey.

"I find it interesting that you're wearing that bracelet on your arm, yet you're stressing over a Christmas tree," Jessica commented.

Kelsey looked down at her wrist, where her new diamond bracelet sparkled. Then she looked at Jessica.

"I didn't want the bracelet. I wanted the tree," Kelsey replied.

Jessica giggled. "I think you're missing my point, Kels," Jessica said.

"No, I get it, Jess," Kelsey said, attempting to explain. "I don't know, I guess I was really disappointed when I thought that I wasn't getting a tree, and I'm feeling kind of guilty about that."

"There's nothing wrong with wanting things occasionally, Kels."

"I know."

"Do you?" Jessica asked.

Kelsey sighed. "I've been given a lot lately. Two houses, more jewelry than I can wear, and of course, a wonderful husband. It just seems like I should be a little grateful."

"You are grateful, aren't you?"

"Maybe I meant satisfied."

Jessica fixed Kelsey with a serious look. "I think that you need to be kinder to yourself. You and I both know that the boys use the trees to commemorate special occasions in our lives. Maybe you wanted a tree, because deep down you knew that if Tyler had one made for you, that would mean that getting married to you was important to him."

Kelsey felt tears coming to her eyes, and Jessica gave her a hug.

"Of course getting married to you was important," Jessica added. "You're so silly."

Tears streamed out of Kelsey's eyes, and down her face.

"I'm ruining my makeup," she whispered as the tears fell.

"I'll fix it," Jessica said, continuing to hold Kelsey.

"Why is it so hard for me to accept that Tyler loves me?" Kelsey said softly, breaking away from Jessica, and wiping her eyes with the back of her hand.

"I don't know, but he does. Right now, he's somewhere in this house, impatiently waiting for his beautiful wife to come back to him," Jessica said.

Kelsey sniffled. "I think I'm less beautiful now," she joked.

Jessica picked up her phone. "That's easy to fix," she said, sending a message. "But the way that you think about yourself, that's a little harder."

Kelsey sighed deeply.

"You have got to work on this," Jessica said seriously. "In less than an hour, we're going to walk into the convention center, and everyone is going to want to meet the gorgeous, confident Kelsey Olsen."

"I think she's on Instagram," Kelsey joked.

Jessica frowned at her. "Really, Kels."

"I know, Jess," Kelsey said. "I know how important this is to Tyler."

"It should be important to you," Jessica replied. "You need to be sure of yourself if you're going to try to balance being Mrs. Tyler Olsen and a super-lawyer every day."

Kelsey picked up a tissue, and dabbed at her eyes as she glanced in a mirror.

"Do you think he loves me?" Kelsey blurted out.

"Are you kidding me?"

"No. Maybe. I don't know Jess."

"Kelsey, what's wrong?"

"I'm afraid I'm going to disappoint him. He's worked so hard for us to be together, and every day I wake up in this fantasy world that Tyler has created for me. And I'm afraid that I'm going to screw it up for him."

"What could you do?" Jessica asked, confused.

Kelsey considered Jessica's question. Deep down, Kelsey knew exactly what she could do, what she was capable of, because she had done it once before. She had let her emotions be her guide, instead of her reason, and she had ended up in a totaled car, pinned under a tree.

But Kelsey knew this was different. She was a different person, at a different time. However, she still felt like emotions could overwhelm her once more, if she didn't maintain complete control. And that was her fear. Losing control.

"I could say the wrong thing. Talk to someone I shouldn't. Get caught by the paparazzi."

"Doing what? Going into Starbucks? You don't do anything," Jessica replied.

Kelsey sighed. Jessica had a point.

"I bet that you haven't done anything that you would be embarrassed to have splashed over the internet since you were sixteen years old. You're too type A. "

Kelsey smiled at the thought. Jessica was right. The only time that she was doing things that she wouldn't want others to know about, she was in bed with Tyler, and he was doing those things with her.

"Kelsey, you're human. We all are. Tyler loves you just the way you are. You don't have to be perfect for him, or for the press. Just be yourself. Your confident, wonderful self."

Kelsey nodded. "I'll try. Thanks, Jess," she said, hugging Jessica as Jade walked back into the room escorting Kelsey's makeup artist.

Kelsey looked at her makeup artist sheepishly, as the artist studied Kelsey's makeup.

"Sorry," Kelsey said.

"We're going to be late," Jade sighed.

An hour later, Kelsey was all smiles as she and Tyler walked into the Tactec holiday party, hand in hand.

"You look so beautiful," Tyler whispered to her for the third time since he had seen her.

"Thanks. I love you," Kelsey replied.

"I love you too," Tyler said. Kelsey knew that he did. The conversation with Jessica had helped, because slowly Kelsey was understanding where she was going wrong. She wasn't her past, and she needed to focus on her present so she and Tyler could get to their future.

It was OK for Kelsey to want things, for her to be in love, and for her to live this life with Tyler. Tyler believed this, and Kelsey knew that she needed to believe this too.

"Are you ready to meet a few people?" Tyler asked her.

"Sure," Kelsey said.

"OK," Tyler replied. Holding her hand, he steered her to a group standing with Bob Perkins.

It was forty-five minutes before they finally made it to their table. At previous Tactec parties, Tyler and Ryan had made it their goal to slide into their seats mere minutes before the program started, skipping the cocktail party before the main event. And in fact, Kelsey had seen Ryan and Jessica walk in only a few minutes earlier. But as the next Tactec CEO, Tyler now had to be seen by the right people at the company, and show that he was the right person to lead them.

Just as Tyler was holding out Kelsey's seat for her, Kelsey heard someone call Tyler's name.

"Hi, Dane," Tyler said, shaking the man's hand as Kelsey sat. She looked wide-eyed at the younger man who stood next to Dane. "Kelsey, this is Dane Sobol. He's in charge of our new ventures group. They work on our collaborations with other companies."

"It's nice to meet you," Kelsey said, shaking Dane's hand.

"You too. Tyler, have you met Chase Holland?" Dane asked. And Kelsey watched her husband in interest.

It had been slightly more than a year earlier when Jessica had set Kelsey up on a blind date with Chase. Jessica was furious with Tyler at the time, because he had broken up with Kelsey. Less than 24 hours after the date, Ryan had found out who Chase was, and told him that Kelsey was dating Tyler. Afraid for his job, Chase had stayed away from her. However, in the process, Ryan had told Tyler Chase's name.

"I haven't," Tyler said, shaking Chase's hand — and from his tone, Kelsey knew that a year later, Tyler still remembered Chase's name and relationship to Kelsey. "It's good to meet you."

"Same," Chase said awkwardly. He glanced at Kelsey, who gave him a pleasant smile.

"This is my wife, Kelsey," Tyler said to Chase.

"Hi, Chase," Kelsey said, extending her hand.

"Mrs. Olsen," Chase replied, shaking it. Kelsey felt bad for him, but at this moment, at least, she knew she wasn't at fault. This awkwardness was a result of Jessica and Ryan's meddling.

Dane, who was blissfully unaware of the dynamics in front of him, continued. "Chase has just been promoted. He'll be working on our relationships with movie studios."

"Congratulations, Chase. That's a very big responsibility. Are you prepared for it?" Tyler asked him.

Chase swallowed nervously. "I think so."

Dane slapped Chase on the back. "Of course he is."

"That's great," Tyler said. "I'll be curious to see what collaborations you'll be doing in the next six months."

Chase gave Tyler a weak smile.

"You won't be disappointed," Dane said to Tyler. "We'll have some exciting things planned. Are you enjoying working with Bob?"

"Bob's a wonderful mentor," Tyler replied.

"While you're in his office, see if you can get us some more money," Dane said. "I don't want him cutting our budget next year."

"I'll try, but as you know Bob's always looking for a solid return on investment. That's hard to quantify with collaborations," Tyler said.

"You get us the money, we'll show you the R.O.I.," Dane said.

"I'll see what I can do."

"Good enough. It was great seeing you tonight," Dane said breezily. "Lovely to meet you, Kelsey."

Kelsey gave him a nod as Dane steered Chase away from the table. She suspected that they had more people to butter up. Tyler sat in the chair next to her.

"Don't punish Chase," Kelsey said without preamble.

"What do you mean?" Tyler said innocently.

"I know you know who he is," Kelsey said firmly.

"And?"

"And it's not his fault that he went on a date with me. Jessica put him up to it," Kelsey said.

"Ignorance is no excuse in the law," Tyler said, taking a drink of water.

Kelsey frowned. "Be nice," she pouted.

Tyler lifted her hand and kissed it. "I'll take it under advisement, counsel," he replied.

"How's it been going?" Ryan asked, as he and Jessica sat at the table.

"Wonderful, we just met Chase Holland," Tyler said, looking directly at Jess, who looked away.

Ryan laughed. "Did you really? What was that like?"

"Kels?" Tyler asked her.

"A little awkward," Kelsey admitted.

"Anything to add, Jess?" Tyler asked her.

"It's water under the bridge, Tyler," Jessica said, looking at him.

"As long as you're sure," Tyler replied.

"Dane's been nagging Bob for a budget increase," Ryan commented. As the Chief Marketing Officer of Tactec, in addition to his other duties, Kelsey knew that Bob was responsible for the New Ventures department's budget.

"He's not going to get it," Tyler said. "Bob's looking for places to cut, not money to spend."

"Bob and Lisa were talking about the budget at brunch last weekend," Ryan continued. "Marketing's going to take a big hit."

"Why?" Kelsey asked.

Ryan laughed, "As far as Lisa's concerned, the most visible marketing for the company during the past two quarters was been on Instagram with Tyler's wife, and my children."

"Direct quote," Jessica added.

"Are the babies getting paid? Kelsey is," Tyler asked Ryan.

"Lisa said she would throw some money in their college fund," Ryan replied. "It doesn't matter, Jess likes to post for them."

"It's cute," Jessica said.

"And quite lucrative for the company," Tyler added.

"Yeah, Lisa's pretty happy about that. But I think that Dane won't be," Ryan mused.

The program started, and Lisa and Bob were sharing the spotlight. As was usual for the holiday party, the tone was upbeat and positive — a recognition of the year's accomplishments, along with hints of the plans for the future.

Kelsey glanced around the room. Tactec had grown since Kelsey's first year, and the number of employees in attendance had grown as well. She did note, however, that one demographic in the audience seemed to have declined. Now that both of the scions of the Tactec founders were married, many Tactec employees seemed to have left their college- and graduate-school-aged daughters at home.

As Lisa and Bob returned to their table, and three members of the executive team took the stage, two couples joined Kelsey's table. Zach arrived with a glowing Reina, and to Kelsey's surprise, Alana sat down next to Brandon. They were holding hands.

"You're late," Ryan said to them.

"We were in the back, talking to my parents," Zach said, as Reina gave Kelsey a wave across the table. Kelsey waved back, and noticed that her new diamond bracelet sparkled in the candlelight. She put her hand back down in her lap.

Jess nudged Kelsey, and she glanced over at Alana as she did so. Kelsey's eyes followed Jessica's. Brandon, who never looked particularly happy, was beaming .

"What's with him?" Jessica whispered. Kelsey shrugged.

"So where's Bob's date?" Zach asked Ryan.

"He didn't bring one this year," Ryan said unconcernedly.

"That's weird," Zach said.

"He doesn't always," Tyler replied.

"I was hoping to see a celebrity," Zach joked.

"Maybe next week," Tyler replied, his brown eyes returning to the stage.

Kelsey, in the meantime, looked around the table. This year's theme was striking, very different than years past. A miniature pine tree sat in the middle of the table, decorated and surrounded by bronze-and-turquoise ornaments. When they had been getting dressed, Kelsey and Jess had been surprised by the color of their evening gowns, which were both lovely shades of aqua, but now it made perfect sense.

As the executive team discussed Tactec's plans for the upcoming year, and they were served salads, Kelsey saw Ryan nudge Jessica and point down at his phone. Jess smiled at him, then picked up Ryan's phone and showed Kelsey what they were looking at. The twins were together in one crib, sleeping peacefully.

"Adorable," Kelsey said to the proud parents. Tyler glanced over at her words, and saw the babies. He gave Kelsey a wink.

"So it's your turn soon?" Jessica asked curiously.

"Not a chance," Kelsey said with a giggle.

The Tactec party proceeded much like the last one that Kelsey had attended. Zach's parents joined them at the table, dinner was served, and a jazz singer serenaded them into the night. Lisa and Bob both dropped by the table to greet them, and during dessert, Kelsey and Tyler rose once again to say hello to a few more Tactec employees.

As the party began to wind down, Brandon, who had been beaming all night said, "Let's go hang out after this is over."

Jessica looked at Brandon in surprise.

"I need to get back to the babies," she demurred.

"Just for a few minutes, Jess," Ryan said to her. "They're sleeping anyway."

"You're going?" Jessica said to Kelsey.

"Sure," Kelsey said. Although she rarely dealt with Brandon, she knew that all the boys considered him a friend.

"OK," Jessica said, lifting up her phone. "I'll let Audrey know we'll be a little late."

Kelsey turned to Tyler, who nuzzled her ear. She laughed in delight as he gave a kiss on the cheek.

"We're going to say goodbye to my parents," Zach said as he and Reina stood up. As usual, Zach's parents had spent most of their time at the party walking around the room, meeting people.

Brandon and Alana stood as well.

"Us too," Brandon said, and the couple left the table.

"OK night?" Tyler asked Kelsey.

"It was fine," Kelsey said, looking into his sparkling brown eyes.

"It will be better once we're in bed," Tyler said quietly to her, and Kelsey's insides flipped.

"Tyler," she scolded as her phone buzzed with a notification. She gave him a smile as she picked it up. Kelsey looked down. The Kelsey Olsen Instagram account had posted a picture. Kelsey opened Instagram and looked at the post that had been made in her name. It was a repost from Jessica's Instagram.

Kelsey laughed, and showed the picture to Jess. "That was fast," she said.

Jessica giggled. "Daisy's working hard tonight," she commented.

Kelsey looked back at the photo that Jessica had taken moments ago. It was delightful. Jessica had managed a great photo of the exact moment that Kelsey had been laughing as Tyler kissed her cheek.

"Nice one, Jess," Tyler said looking at the photo. He kissed his bride's cheek again.

"Daisy's here," Kelsey said to Jess. She and Tyler had run into her earlier. Although Daisy technically worked for Becks, Kelsey assumed that she had been invited to the party so she could post about the evening. As Kelsey ran her finger down Kelsey's Olsen's Instagram posts, she realized her assumption was correct.

"Of course," Jessica said. "You'll be lucky if she's not invited to Lisa's for Christmas, so she can post about all of the wonderful Tactec presents under the tree."

Tyler laughed. "Christmas would be too late. Then there's not enough time for people to go out and buy the products."

"Yeah," Kelsey added, "I'm sure there will be a post of me wrapping Tactec presents in a few days."

"Lisa really doesn't pay you enough," Tyler noted, as the other two couples returned to the table.

"Let's go," Brandon said brightly.

A few minutes later, Kelsey sat next to Tyler in Lisa's red Karmann Ghia as they drove through the streets of Bellevue. Although Martin had driven them to the event, the Karmann Ghia had been waiting in the parking lot for them.

"So did you have any thoughts about the evening?" Tyler asked her.

Kelsey considered the question.

"I was surprised that it went as smoothly as it did," she said. "You seem to be more popular than you've been leading me to believe."

"I have a few allies," Tyler said. "But mostly I think it's because everyone wants more money in their budget, and they think I'll talk Lisa into it."

"Isn't next year's budget already set?" Kelsey asked. "I would think that everyone would already needed to have done next year's planning."

"Every department is allocated an amount based on 75% of next year's total budget, but Lisa and Bob hold back the final 25% until after fourth-quarter results are finalized. That's what everyone is fighting over right now."

"But it's not going to Marketing."

"No. Your boyfriend is out of luck."

Kelsey laughed. "You're my boyfriend. You're always so jealous about nothing."

"I'm jealous about you. Not nothing," Tyler replied.

"There's nothing to be jealous over. I'm your Kelsey," she said, rubbing Tyler's arm. He shifted gears, and Kelsey noted the smile on his face. "So what's up with Brandon?"

"What do you mean?" Tyler asked innocently.

"Tell me," Kelsey said.

"You'll see," Tyler replied as they turned a corner.

The couple walked into the vintage industrial restaurant where they were meeting the others a few minutes later. Kelsey had got no other information out of Tyler about Brandon, although she had spent the rest of the ride trying.

Kelsey sat in the chair that Tyler pulled out for her, and he sat next to her, taking her hand into his own. The group stood out in the restaurant, as they still wore their evening gowns and tailored suits. Most of the rest of the crowd was weekend casual.

"I love your shoes," Reina said, pointing to Kelsey's feet.

"Thanks," Kelsey said. She and Jessica were wearing variations of the same designer. Kelsey's were a medley of beaded vines and silk flowers, while Jessica's were adorned with a beaded-silk-flower bow. Both pairs were delicate and exquisite.

"What are we having?" Zach asked picking up the menu.

Tyler slid a menu towards himself and Kelsey.

"Mac and cheese," Tyler said. "And sliders."

"Someone wasn't happy with tonight's menu," Zach commented as Brandon and Alana walked up.

"I'm tired of salmon," Tyler replied. Kelsey knew his statement was true. Tyler had left three-quarters of his salmon on his plate at the Tactec dinner. No wonder he was hungry.

"I want dessert," Jessica piped up.

"Something non-vegan?" Brandon asked her with a grin.

"The animals matter," Ryan said. "As does Jessica's health."

"You can cook for me tomorrow," Jessica said with a wave of her hand. "I want the chocolate-chip cookie."

"Make it two," Kelsey said.

Orders placed, Kelsey leaned her head cozily on Tyler's shoulder as they talked.

"What are you doing for Christmas, Reina?" Jessica asked her. Jessica's new diamond earrings sparkled in the dim light.

Reina glanced at Zach before answering.

"I'm going to Yokohama to visit my grandfather," she said. "We go every year."

"When are you going to take Kelsey to Japan?" Zach asked Tyler.

Tyler shrugged. "Soon, I hope. Maybe once Chris settles down. Right now, the best I can offer Kelsey is San Francisco next month. I need to go for Tactec, but we can make a weekend out of it."

"That would be great," Kelsey said. She loved San Francisco, and she really wanted to check on Morgan. She and Morgan had been discussing the possibility of Kelsey flying down, and now here was Kelsey's chance.

"I think we should go to Canada during the holiday," Ryan said.

"Use your new visa?" Brandon asked with a smirk.

"I did my time," Ryan replied. "Now we can take the babies up."

"Let's go," Jessica said, smiling at Kelsey. Kelsey nodded. With two weeks off for the holidays, she knew that there would be plenty of time for a trip to Vancouver.

"Are you doing something special for the holidays, Alana?" Kelsey asked.

Alana shook her head. "I'll be working," she said. "Collins Nicol isn't as nice as Bill Simon. I don't get two weeks off."

Tyler snickered. "Nice," he said under his breath.

"Kelsey's earned it," Jessica said. "She works so much more than we do at Tactec."

"Ryan's about to find out about working," Zach commented.

"Don't remind me," Ryan pouted.

"You only have to work three days a week. Get over it," Tyler said.

"I shouldn't have to go at all. I have babies at home," Ryan said.

"That's why Bob said you only need to work three days a week," Jessica said. "The babies will be fine without you."

"Maybe better," Tyler commented.

"I hope so," Ryan said to Jess, glaring at Tyler.

"Just take them to work," Zach said. "Lisa will love it."

Ryan shook his head. "I'm working in Legal. I don't want the babies to hear all that swearing from the lawyers in the office."

Jessica giggled. "I don't think they'll care," she pointed out.

"I'll think about it," Ryan mused.

The food for the table came, and they started eating.

"I guess no one liked dinner tonight," Jessica commented, looking around the table.

"It was just boring," Tyler editorialized. "This is much better."

"It's really good," Reina said. "Has anyone eaten here before?"

"Brandon and I had our first date here," Alana said.

"That's sweet," Reina said.

Kelsey saw Zach and Tyler glance at each other, but neither of them spoke.

Jessica offered Ryan a bite of her ice cream but he shook his head no.

"It's not vegan," he said to her.

"Oops, sorry," Jessica said, eating it.

"Alana, you aren't hungry?" Kelsey asked. Alana hadn't eaten a bite.

"I'm waiting for chocolate cake," she said. "It's my favorite. But it's taking a while."

"I'm sure it's on the way," Brandon said, glancing at the kitchen. His eyes met Ryan's, then they both looked away from each other.

"Have a bite of my cookie," Kelsey said, gesturing to the portion of dessert on her plate. Alana lifted up her fork and took some of Kelsey's dessert. As she did so, Kelsey spotted their server walking over to their table, with a big smile, holding a slice of cake. She walked up to the table, and placed the cake in front of Alana with a flourish. And Alana gasped.

As everyone around the table looked over, Brandon got to one knee. He removed the engagement ring that was sparkling on top of the slice of chocolate cake.

"Will you marry me?" Brandon asked Alana. She looked back at him in disbelief and nodded.

"Yes," she said softly, and the group burst into applause.

"That was so romantic," Kelsey said as she, Tyler, Ryan, and Jessica headed to their cars a while later.

"I didn't know that Brandon had that in him," Jess commented.

"Zach's next," Ryan said. "Do you know when he's going to propose?"

"Soon, I bet," Tyler said noncommittally.

"When, Tyler?" Ryan pressed.

"Valentine's Day," Tyler admitted.

"Zach never tells me anything."

"Make sure Reina doesn't find out," Tyler warned.

"We probably won't see her before Valentine's day," Ryan pointed out.

"True," Tyler said as they reached the Karmann Ghia. "We'll see you at your house," he said, opening the door for Kelsey.

Kelsey carefully got into the car, adjusting her aqua dress, and Tyler closed her door. He got into the driver's seat, leaned over and kissed Kelsey.

"Thank you for inviting me," Kelsey said. "I had a wonderful night."

Tyler ran his finger down a strand of Kelsey's hair and surveyed her with his sexy brown eyes. Then he leaned over and kissed her again.

"So is Bob going to San Francisco with you?" Ryan asked a while later, as they sat in the game room at the Perkins house. The babies had been checked on, and the foursome had changed out of their dress clothes, and into sweats and pajamas.

"Yes," Tyler replied.

"Why?"

"We need to meet some venture capitalist there. He's got a bunch of startups that he thinks Tactec will be interested in."

Ryan surveyed Tyler with his bright blue eyes.

"They broke up, Ryan," Tyler said to the unasked question. "Stop obsessing about Morgan."

Ryan sighed. "I think Bob's thinking about getting married again. Thanks to Aunt Olena's meddling."

"Bob's always thinking about getting married," Tyler said dismissively. "That's his nature."

"I know," Ryan said.

"Anyway, who's he going to marry?"

Ryan glanced at Kelsey.

"Not Morgan," Kelsey said firmly.

"You obviously haven't seen Miss Hill's social media accounts, Ryan," Tyler added. "I'm not sure she remembers Bob's name."

"Come on, Tyler," Ryan said.

"No, you come on. They broke up months ago."

"They still talk on the phone," Ryan said.

"And you know that how?" Tyler said.

"I have my sources," Ryan replied. "Look, you don't care because Lisa's going to marry Simon. But it's been a long time between wives for Bob, and I know he's thinking about it. I just don't know who he's thinking about."

"He might just pick someone at random," Jessica said. "Hey, you. Want to marry a billionaire?"

"Not funny, Jess," Ryan pouted.

"No, it totally is," Tyler said. "Good one, Jessica. Look Ryan, if you're so concerned, why don't you just ask him?"

"I did. He said that he wasn't planning on getting married. He said he's having too much fun."

"Maybe he is."

"He's not," Ryan replied. "I thought that he was, but Bill told Lisa that Bob spent most of the trip in Arizona complaining about how bored he was. And you know what that means."

"Wife number five," Tyler said to Kelsey. "But he's got to find someone, and you and I know there aren't any likely candidates."

"What about that woman in Arizona? Fiona?"

"She's been around too long. Bob's never married anyone he's dated for more than six months."

"There's always a first time," Ryan said.

"If I were you, I'd look in the current dating pool for the next Mrs. Bob Perkins," Tyler replied.

A half-hour later, after they had said goodnight to the Perkins family, Kelsey breathed deeply.

"Are you sure?" Tyler asked, kissing her collarbone. Kelsey closed her eyes, in bliss. Tyler was teasing her and she was loving it.

"They can't hear us," she replied. "I'm not concerned." She was lying on the bed in the ground-floor guest bedroom in Jessica and Ryan's house.

"I know how shy you are," Tyler said, nibbling her ear.

"I'm not shy tonight."

"I could stop," Tyler said, slowly unbuttoning Kelsey's pajama top.

"You better not," Kelsey replied, pulling him towards her.

The next morning, sunlight streamed into the guest bedroom. Kelsey lay in Tyler's strong arms, and she gently turned the gold band on his ring finger.

"Can I ask you a question?" Kelsey asked.

"Of course, Princess," Tyler said, nuzzling her hair.

"Do you think your therapist helped you?"

"Which one? I've had several," Tyler said.

Kelsey turned in his arms so she could look at him. "Pick one," she said.

"I think the last one did. I'm not sure that I would have gotten my eating disorder under control without his help."

"How did he help you?" Kelsey asked.

Tyler was thoughtful. "He gave me a different perspective on my problems. I was spending a lot of time in my own head, and that wasn't helping me at all."

"So you think therapy is valuable?"

"I think that it has its place. Why do you ask?"

"Just curious," Kelsey said thoughtfully. She closed her eyes and cuddled into Tyler's chest. He tightened his grip around her naked body.

They were silent for a moment, then Tyler asked: "Do you think that you need therapy?"

"Maybe," Kelsey replied.

"Do you want to talk to me first?" he asked.

Kelsey hesitated. "No," she finally said. "I don't think that you'll understand."

"It's about money," Tyler concluded.

"Yep," Kelsey said, although she thought it was about more.

"Jeffrey can arrange one for you. He has a team of them on speed dial."

"He does not."

"Of course he does. It's a necessity. Have you met my parents?" Tyler replied.

Kelsey giggled. "OK, maybe you have a point," she said.

"Are you happy?"

"Yes. Just a little confused."

"Are you sure that I can't help?"

"I'm sure," Kelsey said, stroking his chest.

Tyler kissed her deeply. "Perhaps I can help with something else?" he asked seductively.

Kelsey looked at him and smiled. She pressed her warm body against his. "I'm quite sure you can," she replied, kissing him back.

"Allie, no," Mischa said grumpily as Allie spit mashed peas out of her mouth.

"She doesn't like it," Jessica said, as Ryan wiped Allie's mouth with a soft washcloth. Allie coughed.

"Rory's a fan," Tyler said. Rory was sitting with Audrey, and was happily eating mashed peas.

"It's fine. Let's get some sweet potatoes for Allie," Jessica said, moving the bowl of peas. "She loves those." Mischa stood and headed for the kitchen.

"Do you want to feed Allie, Kels?" Ryan asked as he finished wiping his baby daughter's lips.

"OK," Kelsey said, a little nervously.

"You'll do fine," Jessica said, handing the now-clean Allie to her. Allie gave Kelsey a big smile, and Kelsey gave her a cuddle.

"So how many foods are they up to?" Tyler asked, as Mischa returned with a bowl of mashed sweet potato.

"Those aren't microwaved, are they?" Ryan asked, eyeing the bowl suspiciously.

"Of course not," Jessica said, taking the bowl from Mischa. "I made it myself. I knew Allie was going to hate the peas. They've tried seven foods, Tyler. Rory's liked them all so far, and Allie likes rice, avocado, sweet potatoes, and squash. She cries when she sees a banana, and she doesn't like barley. Here's the spoon, Kels," Jessica said, handing it to her.

Kelsey took a tiny amount of the soft sweet potato onto the spoon and she offered it to Allie. Allie ate it right up.

"At least she won't starve," Jessica commented, as she smiled at Ryan.

Allie opened her mouth for Kelsey, and Kelsey gave her another tiny spoonful.

"It's yummy, right sweetie?" Jessica cooed at Allie. Allie smiled at her mother.

Jessica stroked Allie's auburn hair. "Such a good girl," she said.

"You're a natural, Kels," Ryan said.

"I don't think so," Kelsey replied.

"We need a picture," Jessica said, pulling out her phone. "Tactec's two Instagram stars."

"Rory probably should get in the photo too," Tyler commented. "I wonder what Marketing will be selling with this one," he asked as Jessica took the picture.

"You should know, you've been working with Bob," Jessica said, showing Kelsey the photo.

"The new line of tablets," Ryan said, now holding Rory in his arms, and stroking his back.

"That's probably it," Tyler agreed. "A perfect stocking-stuffer."

"What does that have to do with me feeding Allie?" Kelsey asked, offering the baby more food. Allie ate another bite.

"That's what we pay Marketing for," Tyler said, smiling as Rory grabbed his hand. "I'm sure they'll find a way to tie the two together."

"What's wrong?" Ryan asked Jessica. She frowned as she looked at her phone.

"Hang on," she said, standing up and walking away.

"Can you take Rory?" Ryan asked Tyler. Tyler took baby Rory into his arms, and Allie made a little cry.

"Sorry," Kelsey said to her, giving Allie another spoonful of food. Allie ate it happily.

A few minutes later, Jess and Ryan returned to the table. Jessica sat down, and Ryan put his arm around her shoulders.

"Is everything OK?" Kelsey asked. Allie had finished eating and Kelsey was gently rocking her.

Jessica sighed. "My mom is moving out of Joey's house after the holidays. She's getting her own apartment."

"Oh, Jess, I'm sorry," Kelsey said. Jessica nodded, and Kelsey could see the tears forming in her eyes.

"It will be OK," Ryan said to her, hugging her shoulders. But Jessica was silent.

"She blames herself, doesn't she?" Tyler asked as he and Kelsey drove onto the expressway.

"Jess? Yes, definitely," Kelsey replied. The couple had stayed for another two hours and played with the babies, but it was clear that the news had upset Jessica, and she had been virtually silent during the rest of the visit.

"It's not her fault," Tyler said.

"Of course it isn't, but Jess thinks that if she hadn't married Ryan, her parents would have never broken apart."

"Or it could have just been a matter of time. Something else might have happened to make Jessica's mother assert herself."

"Maybe, but that's not the way Jess sees it. Her brother blames her too, so I don't think she's likely to change her mind."

"If I've learned anything, it's that your parents will do whatever they want to, and there's no point in blaming yourself for their actions."

"Maybe Jess needs a therapist too," Kelsey commented.

"It might help," Tyler replied. "Did you message Jeffrey about yours?"

"I'll talk to her at lunch on Wednesday."

"So soon?"

"No time like the present. Anyway, I'd like to deal with my issues before we show up on Lisa's doorstep. At least I can get started."

"Are you worried about spending the holidays with Lisa?"

"Not really. Considering everything I've heard about fourth quarter, I've been wondering if we'll even see her," Kelsey said.

"You have a point. I think she'll at least be at home on Christmas Day," Tyler mused.

Kelsey thought about Tyler's words. They made her sad. In all of the years that Kelsey had known Tyler, he had not returned to the Olsen home for Christmas. Not once. She knew that Lisa Olsen had made many sacrifices to build Tactec, and Christmas would be just another reminder of those sacrifices. Kelsey just hoped that being there with him would allow Tyler to have the family Christmas that he wanted at the Olsen home, and that Kelsey suspected that he had never truly had.

Kelsey was still thinking about Christmas at Lisa Olsen's house when Jeffrey sat down in front of her desk. As always, he was meticulously dressed, but as sometimes happened, Jeffrey's face told the truth about his day. And today, Jeffrey was clearly stressed.

"So you're all set for Wednesday," Jeffrey said to Kelsey as he skimmed through his tablet. "Did you need Jade to walk you over to the office?"

"No, it's fine. I think I can make it over there without her," Kelsey said. The therapist's office was four blocks away.

"Great," Jeffrey said, without noticing Kelsey's amusement. "Did you need me to purchase any Christmas presents?"

"No, I have them under control," Kelsey replied.

"Do you have any requests for the staff at Ms. Olsen's house?"

"No."

"Any food preferences that Margaret needs to know about?"

"No."

"I'll be interviewing another three women for the position of your assistant before I leave. I apologize that this has taken so long, but I want to find exactly the right person for you."

"I appreciate your help," Kelsey said. "Jeffrey?"

"Yes?" Jeffrey said, looking up at her.

"Are you OK?"

Jeffrey sighed. "I'm fine, Kelsey," Jeffrey said, looking back at his tablet.

"Jeffrey," Kelsey pressed.

"I'm a little concerned about being out of state while you and Tyler are staying with Ms. Olsen," Jeffrey said, looking back up at Kelsey.

"Why?" Kelsey said in surprise.

"Tyler hasn't been at home for a while, and you've never stayed there, and I'm a little concerned about your visit."

"We'll be fine," Kelsey said.

"I'm sure you'll be," Jeffrey said.

Kelsey giggled. "Tyler will be fine too."

"Hmm," Jeffrey said thoughtfully.

"What are you concerned about?" Kelsey asked. She wasn't usually so informal with Jeffrey, but he seemed quite worried.

"One of my roles is to be a bridge between Ms. Olsen and her son. I won't be able to do that from a thousand miles away."

"I'm sure they'll manage to get along," Kelsey said, but as she spoke the words, she realized that she had her doubts too.

"I'll comfort myself with the fact that they have managed to work in the same company for almost eight months without a lawsuit or a demand letter," Jeffrey commented.

Kelsey burst into laughter and Jeffrey gave her a smile.

"That is quite impressive," Kelsey said between laughs.

"You have no idea," Jeffrey commented.

"We'll be fine. Lisa will probably be working a lot, and I'm sure we'll find things to do. You should go and have a nice time with your family, and we'll see you next year," Kelsey said.

"I'm only a plane ride away, so don't hesitate to contact me," Jeffrey said firmly.

"We won't, but thank you," Kelsey replied. "Have a good trip."

"Thank you," Jeffrey replied. "I'll do my best."

After Kelsey said goodbye to Jeffrey, she realized that she had more pieces to the puzzle that was Tyler and Lisa's relationship. Jeffrey knew that his role was that of smoothing the waters between Tyler and Lisa, which meant that Lisa had deliberately hired him for that role.

Kelsey had glimpses of how Tyler felt about his childhood, and she had feelings about his childhood as well. Tyler had grown up surrounded by everything that money could buy, but he lacked the things that it couldn't. A father's love, his mother's time. Tyler missed out on these growing up.

Kelsey hadn't talked to Tyler about going home. Of course they had discussed the basics — where they would stay, what they might do — but Kelsey didn't feel like she understood how Tyler felt about the place he had grown up. Kelsey knew how she would have felt, surrounded by servants and luxury, but without someone there to kiss a scraped knee, or give a warm hug. She would have felt alone and sad, and she would never want to go back home, because those feelings would remain.

But Tyler wasn't Kelsey. He didn't seem to have any concerns about going home except for the risk of being roped into doing work for Tactec. That was what made Jeffrey's comments so interesting to her. He was concerned about the visit as well.

Kelsey considered why. She sorted through Tyler's reactions to his parents. He was rarely sad, but often angry. And when he was angry, he did one of two things. He lashed out at the cause of his anger — which was why Jeffrey's lawsuit joke was just a little too true — or Tyler turned the anger inward, to himself.

As Kelsey thought about Jeffrey's comments, she realized why he was so concerned about not being around, but she also realized why Jeffrey didn't need to be. Kelsey knew that Chris's accident had changed everything for Tyler.

When Tyler was a child, Lisa had been the villain in Tyler's world, because she kept him away from his father. But Tyler the adult knew better. Lisa had made the best of a bad situation that Chris had caused. She did it imperfectly, and sometimes unfairly, but she did it all out of love for her child.

Jeffrey hadn't figured out that Tyler was no longer angry with Lisa, but Kelsey knew the truth. She knew that they could expect a merry Christmas after all.

"Are you sure that we're not going to be here for Christmas?" Jake asked Kelsey.

She too had her doubts. It was 2 a.m. on Tuesday morning, and they were still working. Kelsey had sent Tyler off to get some sleep in one of the conference rooms — as he had refused to let her walk home without him — but she and Jake were still not close to being done.

"Once Bill gets through this week, hopefully we'll be fine," Kelsey said. Bill Simon was in Alexandria, Virginia, preparing to argue a case in just a few hours, as it was 5 a.m. there. He would be arguing in front of the U.S. District Court.

"I feel like this one snuck up on us," Jake said, typing into his computer. He had joined Kelsey in her office in an attempt to stay awake.

"It's a rocket docket, so it snuck up on everyone," Kelsey said, referring to this particular court's reputation for speedy trials. The court had rejected every motion for extensions or delays, and the case had moved from pleadings to trial quicker than Kelsey had ever seen.

Jake yawned. He stopped typing and took a sip from the coffee that was sitting next to him.

"I think I'm going to sleep here tonight," Jake commented. "By the time we're done, there won't be a point in going home. I'll just have to turn around and come back in."

Kelsey looked at the work that was still in front of her. Despite the fact that she only lived five minutes away, she had exactly the same feeling.

Kelsey put her work aside on Tuesday afternoon. It wasn't like it was going to go away, and she needed a break, no matter how small. She and Tyler had finally made it home at 6:15 a.m. — and less than three hours later, Kelsey had returned to the office. Right now she was running on adrenaline, but she knew that she would need to make sleep a priority if she wanted to be functional on Wednesday.

Kelsey took a sip of her latte and picked up her phone. She opened Instagram, and smiled at the top post. Kelsey Olsen was thrilled about her brand new Tactec tablet, with the 20 megapixel cameras, perfect for selfies with the twins.

Kelsey scrolled down a few posts and saw one with Morgan, dressed as a tastefully sexy Santa Claus for a holiday party. Morgan had decided to spend Christmas in San Francisco. She was working on both Christmas Eve and the day after Christmas in order to earn some much-needed overtime pay. One of Morgan's two roommates had moved out, and she and her other roommate had to cover the rent until their new roommate moved in.

Kelsey thought about Morgan and her situation. Kelsey had always had more than Morgan, and now was only different in scope. But as always, Morgan would only accept the help that she wanted to accept. Kelsey knew that Morgan wouldn't take money for rent, or a plane ticket. Yet Morgan didn't stand in the way of Bob Perkins giving money to her sisters for college, or sending over food to her family. In the same way that Kelsey would only accept certain things from Tyler when they were dating, Morgan had her own limits.

Kelsey really wanted to do more, because now she had so much more. She wanted to give Morgan more than token birthday and Christmas gifts. It bothered her that she hadn't made time to create her charitable foundation with Tyler. Kelsey knew that she not only had money, but thanks to Daisy's hard work, she also had a platform with the Kelsey Olsen Instagram page. And Kelsey wasn't using it.

It was so easy for her to focus on work, Tyler and her own life — but at moments like this, when she saw Morgan working so hard, or times like when she was asked for money on the street, Kelsey knew that she needed to focus a little less on her own life, and share a little more with others. The problem was that she wasn't quite sure where to start.

The Olsen and Perkins families both had foundations, and both of the foundations donated to education charities. Additionally, there was the Tactec Foundation, which gave scholarships to deserving students, and supported charities all over the world. Kelsey wanted her and Tyler's foundation to reflect their interests, much like the Perkins Family Foundation reflected Bob's. Kelsey had been inspired by how invested Bob was in the outcomes of the students who participated in the Foundation's programs, so much so that he donated millions of dollars per year to keep them fully funded.

Kelsey had spent a lot of time thinking about what she was most passionate about. She wanted to make a difference to the world, not just with her own work, but also with her money. The thing that gave her pause, and part of the reason that she hadn't gone further, was that she wanted Tyler to want to make a difference too.

Because Tyler had always been a member of the Olsen Family Foundation, he wasn't as interested as Kelsey was in creating a new one. He had said he would go along with whatever she wanted to do, but Kelsey really wanted his input. But considering all of the other things on Tyler's mind, Kelsey thought that she might have to wait a while until he gave it to her.

On Wednesday, Kelsey was still a little tired as she sat in a small office, her new therapist in front of her. They had gone through the pleasantries, and Kelsey had reminded the therapist that she wasn't looking for long-term therapy, but instead she just needed an opportunity to talk. Her therapist, Paula, looked at Kelsey through her black-rimmed glasses, as she spoke. From their discussion over the first ten minutes, Kelsey knew that Paula understood who the people in her life were — now it was a matter of uncovering their true relationship to Kelsey.

"Do you think that you're a bad person, Kelsey?" Paula asked.

"No, but I think that I've done some bad things."

"Did you ever hurt anyone?"

"I hurt my parents."

"You hurt their feelings, I know, but did you ever cause an injury to anyone?"

"I hurt a tree."

"Anyone else?" Paula asked.

"Just myself," Kelsey replied.

"Just?"

"I hurt myself," Kelsey corrected.

"How?" Paula asked. Kelsey knew that she wasn't asking about the physical injury this time, but the emotional one. Kelsey was quiet for a moment before she spoke.

"Because I didn't live up to my own standards," she finally said.

"Why not?" Paula asked, and Kelsey was surprised by the question. She had thought that Paula would ask what the standards were.

"Because it was too hard," Kelsey replied.

"It was too hard to live up to your own standards? You created them," Paula said curiously.

Kelsey considered her words.

"I'm not sure that I did. I think that my mother created most of them."

"And you made them your own," Paula concluded.

"Yes, I think so."

"Why did you make them your own, if they were too hard to live up to?" Paula asked.

"I don't know," Kelsey said, but she began to tear up.

"Your tears make me think that you do know," Paula pressed. Once again, Kelsey thought before speaking.

"I just didn't want anyone to be disappointed with me, but they were. And when I realized that, I felt like since they were disappointed with me, there was no point in trying to do better. So I decided to let them be disappointed, and just have fun," Kelsey said in a rush.

"But it wasn't fun for you."

"No. Because I was still disappointing myself."

"When did you change?"

"I'm not sure I've ever changed."

Paula paused for a moment, and they sat in the silence. Kelsey took a tissue and began to wipe her face. This was hard, harder than she had thought it would be, because in just a few minutes, Kelsey had started to feel the feelings that she had buried for so long. And it was clear to Kelsey that in just that short amount of time, Paula had started to dig toward the root of the problem. And as she had said, Kelsey's tears proved it.

"Are you disappointed with yourself?"

"No, not now," Kelsey said, but she could feel her hesitance in her words. She expected that Paula could hear it in her voice too.

"Do you think that your mother is disappointed with you now?"

"I think she is."

"Why?"

"She doesn't have grandchildren," Kelsey said, but in her heart, she could think of a dozen reasons more.

"Have you asked her?"

"Asked her what?"

"How she feels about you now?"

"No."

"Why?" Paula asked.

"I'm a little scared," Kelsey admitted.

"What if she says that she's proud of you?" Paula asked curiously.

"I won't believe her," Kelsey said flatly. She sat with her words for a moment as she considered her relationship with her mother. Kelsey couldn't remember a time when it wasn't tense, when she didn't feel like she was under Kelly North's microscope. It was a source of frustration for her, the fact that she hadn't successfully made those feelings about being around her mother go away.

"Why does it matter?" Paula asked.

"What does what matter?" Kelsey replied.

"Whether people are disappointed in you."

"Shouldn't it?" Kelsey asked in surprise.

Paula shrugged. "It doesn't to some people," she said.

Kelsey considered this. Frankly, she didn't think it mattered to Tyler. He did what he wanted to do, mindful of his responsibilities, but unwilling to bend because of outside opinion.

Paula continued. "I think that's the core of what you need to get to. Why do you think that you owe other people a certain kind of Kelsey, and why does it bother you so much when you don't deliver?" she asked.

Kelsey thought about Paula's words as she sat at her desk an hour and a half later. She had been unable to think of anything else. In fifty-five minutes, Paula had asked Kelsey to challenge some of her fundamental beliefs. Whether a person owed a duty to those around them to behave in a certain way. Whether it was right to make decisions without factoring in the opinions of others. Whether it was OK to just be alive and be loved.

Kelsey had never asked herself any of these questions. Her life had been a switch which turned from on to off. Previously she hadn't cared at all about the opinions of the world — and when the world had called her on it, Kelsey had switched to caring, perhaps too much. Paula had suggested to Kelsey that perhaps there was a middle ground. One where she could consider the concerns of others, without giving up too much of herself. It was food for thought.

"How did it go?" Tyler asked her that night. They were lying in bed, fingers intertwined. As often happened on work nights, intimacy trumped conversation, so Kelsey was tired as she spoke.

"The therapist was good. She got me thinking."

"Will you go back?" Tyler asked.

"I don't know. Not soon."

"She solved all of your problems in one visit?"

"I didn't hire her to solve my problems. I hired her to give me a direction so I could solve them myself."

"Fair enough. Did she do that?"

"I think so," Kelsey said.

"Are you ready to be Kelsey Olsen now?" Tyler asked.

Kelsey felt a small shock at the name. To her, Kelsey Olsen was an ideal, the person that she needed to be. It was the reason behind the therapist visit — the fact that Kelsey hadn't felt like she had lived up to her role.

"I don't know," Kelsey replied. "It still feels weird."

"To be who you are?" Tyler asked.

Kelsey looked at Tyler's beautiful brown eyes.

"Yes," she admitted. "I love you so much, and I want to be everything for you. Everything you want me to be."

"You already are."

"When you say that, I know it's true, but I don't feel that it is. I need to get my heart and my brain on the same playing field."

"You are Kelsey Olsen. You, not some Instagram page or feature in a magazine."

"I know," Kelsey said, but she sighed. "I just have a lot to think about. Can I ask you a question?"

"Of course."

"Is Lisa proud of you?"

Tyler was quiet for a moment, and Kelsey knew that he was thinking.

"I think so. But to be honest, I don't think that Lisa thinks about the world that way."

"What do you mean?"

"Lisa couldn't care less about me going to Darrow or to Harvard. She doesn't think that becoming a lawyer is a big deal. But I think she would say that she is proud of the fact that I've become my own man, that I've learned how to manage my own life, and that I've created my own family. That's what she wanted for me. For me to be happy." Tyler sighed. "That's why she's meddled so much. She's been trying to engineer a path to my happiness. But unfortunately instead she got in the way. I think she's starting to realize that more."

Kelsey agreed. Despite Kelsey's previous concerns, Lisa Olsen had played a minimal role in their personal lives over the past year, and from talking with Tyler, Kelsey knew that he didn't see her much at work. Now that Tyler was married and working for Tactec, Lisa Olsen seemed content with waiting to see how things worked out.

"Do you want her to be proud of you?" Kelsey asked.

"I don't care. I just want to live my life the way I want to."

"I thought you would say that," Kelsey said, cuddling her head against him.

"Do you think that I have a strange relationship with my mother?" Tyler asked.

"I know you have a strange relationship with her," Kelsey teased. "But that's OK, because she's Lisa Olsen."

"What does that mean?"

"It means that because she runs a corporation, and because you are going to lead that corporation in the future, that your relationship has strains that most mother-son relationships don't. I understand that I will never understand the two of you, and how you have chosen to deal with each other."

"That's an interesting insight," Tyler mused.

"You've never thought of that?"

"No, I have, the fact that we have to relate to each other on different levels. But I guess I haven't really thought about our relationship in terms of choice, at least on her part. I know that I make a lot of choices to deal with her brand of crazy, but maybe she makes choices that help her deal with mine."

Kelsey laughed. "Crazy? That seems a little unfair to both of you."

"What would you call it?"

"I think that the two of you are human, and you have both found yourself in a world that you weren't prepared to deal with, so you're doing your best."

"Tactec was created when I was one, so it's not exactly a new part of my life."

"You didn't know you were going to run it. That's new."

"I suppose."

"It makes a difference in how you and Lisa treat each other," Kelsey said.

"I guess. Why are we talking about me?"

"Because by talking about you, I'm talking about myself. I am also finding myself in a world that I wasn't prepared to deal with."

"And you're doing your best."

"I'm trying," Kelsey said.

"I don't see how you could do better," Tyler said.

"No? I do," Kelsey replied.

"How?"

"It could be effortless. I could roll out of bed and be the fabulous Kelsey Olsen, ready for my close-up," Kelsey said, but as the words came out of her mouth, she couldn't help but laugh.

"I don't think so," Tyler said, holding her.

"You are. You wake up and you're Tyler Olsen."

"The troublesome, spoiled brat of Lisa Olsen. That doesn't require any effort at all."

Kelsey giggled. "That's not how Lisa sees you," she pointed out.

"But that's the thing. I'm allowed to be who I am, but Tactec Marketing has created a Kelsey Olsen that has little or nothing to do with you. So I don't think that you need to mold yourself to fit their vision. I want you to be you, and let them figure their Kelsey out," Tyler said.

"It's hard," Kelsey said. "I want you to be proud of me."

"I'm proud of who you are. The real you. I wouldn't have married the Kelsey Olsen on Instagram."

Kelsey looked at Tyler in surprise. "You wouldn't have? She's perfect."

"She's boring," Tyler replied. "That Kelsey Olsen wouldn't stay up late, getting hot and sweaty with me until 3 a.m. It might mess up her hair. "

Kelsey laughed out loud.

"That's the thing about the pictures. It's not reality. The Tyler Olsen of the media is closer to who I really am because people have gotten to know me. I've done interviews, people who've met me have talked about me, and the Tactec community has watched me grow up as Lisa's son. No one knows you, not even Lisa. So they've created a woman who satisfies their needs, and not mine."

Kelsey smiled at Tyler's words. "So you love me?" she asked.

"Yes, Princess. I love you," Tyler replied.

As always, Bill Simon had closed the office for a two-week holiday, but despite this, Kelsey found herself sitting at her desk on Thursday morning. The rocket docket had struck again, so there was another brief to file, and Kelsey was in charge of it.

Jake had left with his wife and baby to visit his in-laws, and Kelsey knew that she would be visiting her own in-laws beginning tomorrow. Tyler, who had taken his vacation days to match Kelsey's, was downtown having lunch with Marquis. Kelsey knew from talking with Erica that Marquis was unhappy at his law firm, so she suspected that was part of the reason for the lunch. Maybe Marquis wanted to work at Tactec Legal. If so, Tyler was the perfect person to talk to.

Bill walked into her office. "I'm ordering pizza. Do you want anything special?"

"Anything's fine," Kelsey replied as she typed. But Bill didn't move, so Kelsey looked up.

"I'm sorry that you're here today," Bill said. Kelsey wasn't surprised by the comment. Although Bill was unrelenting during the rest of the year, he had always given the associates a two-week holiday at the end of the year, but this was the first time Kelsey had heard of anyone working during what was supposed to be their break.

"It's just one day," Kelsey said.

"I hope so."

"You know where I'll be," Kelsey said with a smile.

"I hope not to have to call on you again," Bill replied. "You need to have your vacation."

"I'm OK," Kelsey said. "It's not a big deal."

Bill sighed thoughtfully. "The law isn't what it used to be," he mused. "There was a time that a handshake meant something."

Kelsey knew what he was referring to. Part of the reason that Bill had always been able to give the yearly two-week vacation was because he had arranged a gentleman's agreement among the law firms he regularly dealt with. Bill would refrain from filing motions against them during the holiday season, and they would do the same. But their latest adversary wouldn't agree, which was why Kelsey was in the office. Who knew what else they would come up with between now and the new year?

"We can handle it," Kelsey said confidently.

"You're a real trooper, Kelsey. Let's get this done, and get you back home," Bill said. "I'll let you know when the pizza is here."

At 5:30 p.m., Kelsey sent Tyler a message from her phone. She was standing in the lobby to make sure that Bill didn't have anything else for her to do.

Are you at home?

Hi, Princess. No, I'm buying Lisa's Christmas present. Are you done?

Yes. Where are you? I'll take you to dinner.

Meet me in the lobby of the Fairmont. I'll be there in five minutes. I love you.

I love you too. Kelsey signed off, and headed for the lobby doors.

Five minutes later, she was in her husband's arms.

"I missed you," Tyler said to her, as he took her hand and they walked across the lobby.

"Me too."

"Is Bill done with you?"

"I think so," Kelsey said, hedging.

"What does that mean?"

"It means that I don't expect to have any more work to do between now and New Year's Day, but I told Bill that I would be available if something comes up," Kelsey explained.

"Let's hope nothing does," Tyler said. "Where are you taking me?" he asked.

Kelsey smiled. "Somewhere you want to go," she replied.

"This was a nice choice, Kelsey. Thank you," Tyler said, giving her a smile from behind his menu.

"We don't have any issues coming here," Kelsey replied. They were sitting in the Italian restaurant where they had had two birthday dinners with Ryan. Each time Ryan had made a birthday wish in the restaurant, the wish had come true. The thought of what Ryan would wish for next made Jess nervous, so she had refused to return.

"Ryan thinks this place is magic," Tyler said, putting his menu aside. "I know what I want," he said.

"Lasagna?"

"Yes. Am I that predictable?"

"No. I want lasagna, but I also want penne. So I was hoping to convince you," Kelsey replied.

"You can have all you want, Princess," Tyler said with a smile. He took Kelsey's hands into his own. "So you had a good day?"

"I just worked. So how's Marquis?"

"Tired of being the only visible minority in Seattle's third-biggest law firm," Tyler replied.

"Is he looking for a new job?"

"I asked him not to. I'm going to need to hire a team at Tactec, so I've asked him to wait until April, and join me."

"But you don't know what you're doing."

"True, but Marquis has a technical background. I'm sure he'll be able to help me. If not, I told him that we would find a place for him in Legal if he wants it."

"Good, I know he's not happy where he is," Kelsey said.

"Tactec should be better."

"I think so," Kelsey said happily. She was sure that no matter which opportunity at Tactec Marquis decided to take, it would be an improvement over his current job. "So what did you buy Lisa?"

"A basket."

"A basket?"

"It was made by a member of the Nisqually tribe around 1910. Lisa will like it," Tyler said.

"Is it child-friendly?" Kelsey asked.

"I guess we'll find out," Tyler replied.

Kelsey giggled. "You don't seem worried."

"It wasn't that expensive. Under three thousand dollars," Tyler replied.

"A bargain," Kelsey said with sarcasm.

"Compared to the Kandinsky I threw in the closet, it's nothing."

"I don't think that's the right comparison," Kelsey said.

"What is?"

"Maybe a twenty-dollar basket from the mall? If you compare a three-thousand-dollar basket to that, you can tell it's a lot of money."

Tyler shrugged, and Kelsey took a sip of her water. She set the glass back down.

"I'm going to lose this fight, aren't I?" she said.

"What fight?"

"The fight to get you to to see that you have a lot of money."

"I know that I have a lot of money. I think the problem is that you can't believe that I have so much," Tyler replied.

"You might have a point," Kelsey admitted. "How much did you spend on my Christmas gift?"

"I'm not going to tell you that."

"Over three thousand dollars?"

"It's a secret," Tyler said, giving her a smile.

Kelsey stood at the foot of her bed the next day, looking at her clothes. Despite the fact that they would be literally fifteen minutes from home — and it would be easy to come back or send someone to pick up whatever she had left behind — Kelsey didn't want to accidentally forget something. Staying at Lisa's felt like a really big deal to her, mostly because she never had.

Kelsey had stayed at both of the Perkins' homes, but never at the Olsen one. Of course she had been inside, given the tour, and even changed clothes in one of the bedrooms — but in some ways Tyler's childhood home still seemed a bit of a mystery.

"Hey," Tyler said, walking into the bedroom and putting his arms around her. "Are you still packing?"

"I am."

"We're just going across the lake," Tyler said as Kelsey settled comfortably against his chest.

"I know, but I want to make a good impression."

"Are you kidding me?"

Kelsey turned in Tyler's arms and looked up at him. He gave her a kiss.

"It's important," Kelsey replied.

"Kels, Lisa's not going to be there ninety percent of the time, and the other ten percent she'll be working. It doesn't matter what you wear, or take with you, for that matter. Anyway, we're married. I'm sure she already has an impression about who you are."

"That's what I'm worried about," Kelsey quipped.

Tyler laughed. "Let's just get in the car and go. I'll tell Jeffrey to pack a bag for you."

"No, wait. I'm almost done," Kelsey said, breaking away from him. "Give me five minutes."

"Five."

"Why are you in such a hurry?" Kelsey asked curiously.

"I'm hungry."

"Eat something here," Kelsey replied.

"I don't want anything that's here."

"You're so spoiled," Kelsey giggled. She took his hand. "I'll find something for you."

Kelsey led Tyler out of the bedroom and into the kitchen. As always, it was bright and tidy, although neither of the home's occupants ever did any cleaning. The clean house was Mariel's handiwork, and Kelsey was grateful for it.

Kelsey looked around the kitchen, with a little confusion. The counters were bare, missing the full fruit bowl that usually sat there. She opened the refrigerator.

"There's nothing here," she said in surprise. Although she and Tyler ate out regularly, there was usually a nice selection of food in the refrigerator, thanks to Jeffrey. But the gleaming shelves were bare.

"Mariel went back to Tennessee for the holiday last night. Jeffrey had her clean out the fridge before she left."

Kelsey had to admit that it made perfect sense. As usual, they had eaten dinner in the office last night, and this morning Tyler had called down to the restaurant and had brunch delivered. No wonder there was no food.

"The cupboards must have something," Kelsey said, opening them.

"I finished the cereal that was there before I picked you up on Thursday, and I don't want potato chips."

"Ramen?" Kelsey asked him, holding out a plastic bag of noodles.

"That's for you. I won't eat that."

"That's because you've eaten real ramen, in Japan," Kelsey said, tossing the package back on the shelves. "Fine, you win, I'll hurry."

"I could just run out or order something else."

"No, no, I'll go. I would prefer that you eat something healthy instead of restaurant food again," Kelsey said, giving him a kiss. "Five minutes."

"Thanks for taking your vacation early, so you could be here now," Tyler said to Margaret. He and Kelsey were sitting at the kitchen counter in Lisa's house, eating Brazilian rice and beans. They had gone straight to the kitchen from the car.

"I was happy to do so. It's not every Christmas that you come home, and this year you brought a guest." Margaret gave Kelsey a smile, and Kelsey smiled back.

"Everyone else left town, though. It's going to be quiet," Tyler mused, before he took another bite of food.

"Mariel left yesterday, Jeffrey leaves tonight, Conor went home on Tuesday, and Jade's on her way to Columbia with Carlos," Margaret said, counting on her fingers.

"Carlos?" Kelsey asked Tyler. "Carlos the bodyguard from San Francisco?"

"He and Jade have been going out for years," Tyler said. "I guess you didn't know that."

"No," Kelsey said.

"They started going out, and he trained her to be a bodyguard," Tyler said.

"I had no idea."

"I'm sure that you'll learn more about everyone's lives than you want to know while we're here," Tyler commented.

"How long are you staying?" Margaret asked.

"At least a night," Tyler teased.

"Really, Tyler," Margaret said, frowning.

"No idea. I might want to go home."

"This is your home," Margaret replied.

"Home is wherever Kelsey is," Tyler said.

"She's here now."

"We might pick a different home if Lisa has a bunch of work for me to do," Tyler replied.

"We'll be here at least a week, Margaret," Kelsey said, ending the battle.

Tyler glanced at Kelsey doubtfully. "If you're sure," he commented. Kelsey giggled.

As they were finishing their meal, Tyler said, "Athena. Locate Lisa."

"Lisa is in the living room."

"She's here?" Tyler said to Margaret.

Margaret shrugged. "She wasn't when you arrived," she replied.

"We should go say hi," Kelsey said to Tyler.

"Finish up, and we'll go," he said. Kelsey took another bite of her food, but she realized that she had suddenly lost her appetite. *Nerves*, she thought, putting her fork down.

Tyler finished the food on his plate, then stood up. Kelsey joined him.

"Thanks, Margaret," Tyler said.

"Yes, thank you," Kelsey added.

"You're welcome," Margaret said with a smile. "It's good that you're home."

"Hi, Mom," Tyler said, as he led Kelsey into the living room a few minutes later.

"Tyler!" Lisa said with delight. "Hello, Kelsey."

"Hi," Kelsey said distractedly. She was looking around the living room in complete awe. It was a Scandinavian winter wonderland, full of red and white. There was a giant Christmas tree that was covered in bright red ornaments and tiny Norwegian flags. Mini Christmas trees alternated with stacks of presents on the side tables, and even the sofa pillows had holiday motifs.

"Did an Ikea explode in here?" Tyler asked as he gave his mother a kiss.

Lisa scowled at him. "We didn't decorate for you," she commented.

"It's beautiful," Kelsey said honestly.

"Thank you, Kelsey," Lisa said pointedly. Tyler grinned at his mother, and he and Kelsey sat down in the soft chairs opposite her. Kelsey wasn't surprised to see that there were papers on the coffee table and a Tactec laptop in Lisa's lap.

"How long have you been here?" Lisa asked, putting the computer to the side. "I saw your car outside, but I thought you might have walked over to see Ryan."

"We were with Margaret. We've only been home about a half hour," Tyler said. "You could have asked Athena where we were," he commented. Kelsey heard a small chime as Athena heard her name.

"I figured that you would turn up," Lisa said. "Anyway, she's not always right."

"Still?" Tyler said.

"In the house, if she has the location of both the phone and the person, she still sometimes chooses the phone. It's kind of annoying."

"Why not just always have her choose the person?" Tyler asked.

"Because if someone is moving, sometimes she'll say something unhelpful like, 'I can't find that person', which is not something a parent wants to hear. They'll figure it out," Lisa said with a wave of her hand.

"I didn't know Athena could find people at all," Kelsey commented.

"She normally can't. They're testing the prototype here," Tyler said to Kelsey. "It's kind of intrusive, because it requires a camera in every room." A look passed between mother and son, and Tyler added, "I'll keep that in mind."

Lisa rolled her eyes and sighed. "So," she said, changing the subject, "what will the two of you do while you're here?"

"Just relax, I hope," Tyler said. "I'd prefer not to look at any spreadsheets."

Lisa laughed. "You may get your wish, we're almost done. We didn't do any major acquisitions this year, so accounting has managed to keep up."

"Good," Tyler said. "Otherwise, Ryan asked Kelsey and me to babysit one afternoon, so I guess we'll do that."

"Babysit?" Lisa asked curiously.

"He's giving Audrey and Mischa a break before they leave for Taiwan, but he also wants to take Jess out so they can go Christmas shopping. So we'll watch them that day."

"Audrey and Mischa aren't leaving for a month," Lisa said.

"I think that Ryan thinks that they need a break."

Lisa laughed. "From Allie? She's adorable."

"It's the contrast with Rory," Tyler said. "They've started flipping coins to decide who is in charge of Allie on a given day."

Lisa frowned. "You're kidding."

"That's what Ryan said."

"Maybe we should think about bringing someone else in," Lisa said thoughtfully.

"Maybe. Ryan's afraid that they'll stay in Taiwan and not come back after Chinese New Year," Tyler said.

"I'll talk to him and Jess," Lisa said. "Athena, remind me to talk to Ryan about the nannies tonight at 9."

"Reminder set," Athena replied.

"So what are you working on now?" Tyler asked.

"Just finalizing next year's budget," Lisa said. "Anyone you want to make a pitch for?" she asked.

Kelsey looked at Tyler, thinking about Dane's request.

"No," Tyler replied.

"Not even acquisitions? You and Bob are going to probably hear about some interesting ones when you're in San Francisco."

"If you decide that there's an acquisition you want to make, you'll make space for them in the budget," Tyler replied.

Lisa laughed. "That's true," she replied. "Kelsey, how's your work?"

"Busy," Kelsey replied. She suspected that Lisa already knew everything she needed to know about Simon and Associates, but Lisa continued.

"I understand that you're the only IP lawyer at the moment. How is that?"

"Terrible. Tell your boyfriend to hire someone else," Tyler piped up.

"My boyfriend does what he wants to do," Lisa replied.

"Is he going to ask you to marry him?" Tyler asked out of the blue.

Lisa looked surprised. "I don't think so," she said.

"You haven't been talking about it?" Tyler asked her.

"No," Lisa replied, and as she did, Kelsey thought she understood why Tyler had thought that Bill and Lisa were going to get engaged over the holiday. One of his spies in the house must have overheard something.

"You're sure?" Tyler pressed.

"I'm sure," Lisa said sincerely. "Anyway, you'll be the first to know."

"What do you mean?" Tyler asked curiously.

"Bill said that he would tell you first," Lisa said. "He's still unhappy about how you found out we were dating, so he wants to be transparent with you."

From the tone in Lisa's voice, it was clear that Lisa didn't agree with Bill Simon on this point, but she said nothing more.

"Is he going to ask for my permission?" Tyler asked.

Lisa peered at Tyler. "He didn't say that," she said.

"I see," Tyler said with a small pout.

"Would you give it?" Lisa asked.

"We'll see," Tyler replied, noncommittally.

"Well, it doesn't matter, it's not likely to happen any time soon," Lisa replied. "We're just getting to know each other again."

"You used to live together," Tyler said.

"Twenty-plus years ago. Things have changed," Lisa said.

"Do you want to get married?" Tyler asked.

"Why are we having this conversation?" Lisa asked him.

"Do you want to get married?" Tyler repeated.

"Not today," Lisa replied with sarcasm.

"Come on, Mom."

"I don't know Tyler, I haven't thought about it."

"Really?"

"I have too many other things to think about. I don't need to be thinking about getting married," Lisa replied.

"Good," Tyler said. Lisa laughed.

"Do you want me to get married?" Lisa teased.

"I think you know the answer to that," Tyler replied.

"You're married," Lisa pointed out.

"And?"

"Newly-married people always think that single people should get married," Lisa said.

"I don't think that," Tyler replied. "I'm just happy that I'm married," he added, giving Kelsey's hand a squeeze. She smiled at him.

"Well, I'm not getting married any time soon," Lisa said with finality. "So don't worry about it."

"I'll try," Tyler replied.

"Is there a camera in here?" Kelsey asked Tyler a few minutes later. They had left Lisa to her work in the living room, and gone up to Tyler's childhood bedroom.

Tyler shook his head. "There's a sensor in the hall that syncs with the hallway camera. This is why Athena is having so many problems with location. The engineers are trying to balance privacy with functionality, and they are having a hard time." Tyler put his arms around Kelsey's waist. "Why did you ask about the camera? Did you have something in mind?" he asked nuzzling her neck.

"No," Kelsey blushed.

"We don't have anything else to do," Tyler said.

"We could go see Ryan and Jess."

"They'll be there later," Tyler said, kissing her.

"Should we locking ourselves in a bedroom in the middle of the day?" Kelsey asked.

"Don't tell me that I'm going to have to take you to a hotel again."

Kelsey giggled. "No, it's OK. I'm just wondering how things work in the Olsen house."

"Work is the correct word," Tyler said. "Lisa works, everyone else works, and we do whatever we want."

"Because we're on vacation."

"Exactly," Tyler said.

"So what do you want to do?" Kelsey asked, appeased by his words.

"I think," Tyler said, kissing her collarbone, "we have some work of our own to do."

Kelsey woke up a while later, surrounded by Tyler's arms. She snuggled into his chest, and he sighed happily.

"I like that kind of work," Kelsey said, opening her eyes to look at him. The room was dark, and Kelsey realized that the sun had set.

"Me too," Tyler said, giving her a kiss.

"Athena, what time is it?"

"It's 5:05 p.m.," Athena replied.

"Do you want to go over to Ryan's for dinner?" Tyler asked.

"Are we invited?" Kelsey asked.

"We're always invited. But there won't be any meat," Tyler replied.

"That's fine," Kelsey said thoughtfully.

"What are you thinking about?" Tyler asked, brushing her hair with his hand.

"I'm thinking about how lonely you must have been," Kelsey said, more honest than she had meant to be. She had noticed how silent Tyler's bedroom was, how far away from the other parts of the house where the staff worked. She imagined when he was up here, the rest of the world must have felt very far away.

"I got used to it," Tyler said, and Kelsey heard no bitterness in his voice. His loneliness as a child, like everything else, was just another thing he had overcome.

"Did Ryan come over a lot?"

"Sometimes. When we were younger. He liked to stay here when Bob traveled."

"I imagine so," Kelsey said. She knew that Bob Perkins's home had fewer staff members than Lisa's.

"I don't know, I guess I'm used to the quiet now," Tyler said. "Does it bother you?"

"It's not the quiet. It's the isolation. The house I grew up in is so small that if someone else was home, you pretty much knew. But here, I wonder if anyone's even here."

"Athena, who's in the house?" Tyler asked.

"Lisa, Kelsey, Ryan, Rory, Margaret, Rohan, Aiden, Jennifer, Lou, and Farah."

"Eleven people, yet I hear nothing," Kelsey commented.

"You hear me," Tyler said, giving her a kiss.

"You know what I mean."

"I do," Tyler said.

"Let's get up and go say hi to Ryan," Kelsey said, sitting up.

"Kelsey," Tyler said, running his hand down her back.

"Yes?" she said turning toward him.

"I'm glad you're here with me," Tyler said. Kelsey smiled, leaned down and gave him a kiss.

A quick shower and a few minutes later, Kelsey and Tyler walked into the kitchen. Ryan was standing in the kitchen with Margaret, while Rory lay in a bassinet on the floor, looking up at a mobile.

"Hey, bro," Ryan said.

"We were just about to invite ourselves over for dinner," Tyler said. He lifted Rory out of the bassinet.

"We'd love to have you," Ryan said. "We just came over so Margaret could help me with my aquafaba."

"Your what?" Kelsey asked.

"It's the vegan version of egg whites," Margaret said. "You make it with garbanzo bean water."

"OK," Kelsey said. She had never heard of it.

"What are you making?" Tyler asked as he rocked Rory.

"Chocolate mousse," Ryan said.

"Sounds good. What's for dinner?" Tyler asked him.

"Pizza."

"Margaret, we're going to Ryan's for dinner," Tyler said.

"Do you want to join us?" Ryan asked her.

"No, I'll stay here. Lisa has plans, so I'll make the stock I'll need for Christmas dinner."

"Where is Lisa going?" Tyler asked.

"Don't you mean, who is she going with?" Margaret asked in amusement.

"That was my next question.'

"She's going to the Paynes' house, to have dinner with Keiko Payne," Margaret replied.

"They're talking."

"They've been talking. Just not a lot," Margaret said.

"Why is she going tonight?" Tyler asked.

"You sure are curious," Margaret commented.

"I want to know if it has to do with Zach," Tyler said.

"I think so. Some wedding planning seems to be in the air," Margaret said.

"As long as it's not Lisa's wedding," Tyler commented.

"Why don't you like Bill?" Ryan asked.

"What's to like?" Tyler said.

Margaret laughed. "I bet Lisa could tell you a few things, being that she's dating him."

"Lisa doesn't have great judgment. She married Chris," Tyler replied.

"You're in a great mood. Maybe you should go back to Seattle," Margaret commented.

"I thought this was my home," Tyler said.

"We'll keep Kelsey," Margaret said.

"You want one, you get two," Tyler said.

"I'm almost done, then Tyler and Kelsey can come home with me," Ryan said, ending the discussion. "Tyler, does Rory need a change?"

"No, he's good," Tyler said, bouncing Rory in the air. Kelsey smiled as she watched him. For someone who wasn't in a hurry to have children, Tyler was very good with them. She wondered how long it would be before she was ready to make him a father.

"OK," Ryan said. "So Margaret, do I fold in the chocolate now?"

Fifteen minutes later, they were outside in the cold December air. Ryan carried a large bowl full of chocolate mousse, while Tyler had Rory strapped to his chest in a baby carrier. Rory happily babbled as they walked.

"So what's with you and Margaret?" Ryan asked.

"What do you mean?"

"She seemed a little upset with you."

"It's not me. Margaret's upset because she doesn't know what's going on in the houses. Bill was gone, but now he's back, but she doesn't know what happened, and of course your father is making everyone crazy."

"Bob's not doing anything different than he was before," Ryan said.

"It's been a while since Bob was dating every actress in Hollywood. The staff preferred the Bob who only had two girlfriends."

"As long as Bob's happy, I don't care," Ryan said.

"Is he happy?" Tyler asked.

"He says he is," Ryan replied.

"Does he?"

"We've talked about this, Tyler. Just because you're working with Bob doesn't give you any special insight into his mind. I've known Bob all of my life and he's fine."

"Yeah, but what does fine mean to you? Too busy to notice what you're up to?"

"I'm not up to anything."

"You know what I mean, Ryan."

"No, I don't. I don't see why everyone is so obsessed with who Bob is or isn't dating," Ryan said.

"You were," Tyler pointed out.

Ryan was silent for a moment, and Kelsey suspected that it was because of her presence.

"Well, that's over now," Ryan said. "Let Bob have his fun."

"What are you going to do when he marries one of these starlets?" Tyler asked.

"He's not going to," Ryan said.

"Why are you so sure?" Tyler said, as they passed by the annex that separated Lisa's home from the main building of the Perkins house.

"Because I know my father," Ryan said with finality.

After a peaceful vegan dinner with the Perkins family, and a passionate night with her husband, Kelsey stirred in bed as bright sunlight beamed into their bedroom at Lisa's house.

"Good morning," Tyler said, kissing Kelsey.

"Good morning," Kelsey said happily. "What time is it?"

"Almost 9:30," Tyler replied.

"What are we doing today?" Kelsey asked.

"The same thing we did last night," Tyler replied. Kelsey giggled. Suddenly there was a knock on the door.

"Come in," Tyler said, to Kelsey's great surprise. Automatically, she ducked completely under the covers.

"Good morning," she heard Tyler say.

"Good morning," said a voice she didn't recognize.

"I'll take it from here, thank you," Tyler said. A moment later, Kelsey heard the bedroom door close.

Tyler peeked under the covers. "You can come out now," he said, amusement in his voice. Kelsey did, hesitantly. Before she could ask who had come into the room, she spotted a wheeled cart with two breakfast trays.

"You have breakfast delivered to you in bed?" she said in disbelief.

"Sure," Tyler said. "Sit up," he added. Kelsey did so, and Tyler placed one of the breakfast trays across her lap.

Kelsey looked at him in astonishment.

"Seriously? Every day?"

Tyler took the second tray for himself.

"This is weird?" he asked. He pondered the look on Kelsey's face. "I guess so," he said, removing the top from his plate of food.

"I can't believe that someone delivers breakfast in bed to you. How do they know that you're up?"

"I tell them," Tyler said. Kelsey looked at him curiously. "My phone, Kels," he added.

"Oh," Kelsey said.

Tyler smiled at her. "I'm sorry, I should have told you so you wouldn't be surprised," he said.

"No, it's OK. I just haven't seen your lifestyle in Medina."

"My lifestyle," Tyler commented, taking the top off Kelsey's plate.

"What would you call it?" Kelsey asked, taking a crisp slice of bacon off the plate.

"Our lifestyle," Tyler replied.

Kelsey thought about Tyler's words as she floated in Bob's enormous pool. Tyler was swimming laps next to her, and across the pool, Allie and Rory were having their swimming lesson with their parents and two coaches. This was really her lifestyle, and despite her best efforts, she had to admit that she was starting to get used to it.

Jeffrey had checked in with Tyler on his way to the airport to remind him that he was only a short flight away if he was needed. Margaret had asked Kelsey if she had enjoyed her breakfast, which of course Kelsey had. And Kelsey would be joining Jessica later for a massage, manicure, and pedicure — done with non-toxic, specially sourced, nail polish.

Kelsey looked up at the glass ceiling. She had thought her life ran smoothly living with Tyler in Seattle, but it was nothing compared to Medina. Between security, chefs, nannies, indoor staff, outdoor staff, and who knows who else, Kelsey estimated that there were at least fifty people serving Bob, Lisa, Ryan, Jess, Allie, and Rory. And now, her and Tyler. Six staff members to one person. And it showed.

Everything was immaculate. During the ten minutes they had spent talking to Margaret and returning to their bedroom for their swimsuits, their bed had been made, and the room had been tidied.

Even now, every so often, Bob's butler dropped by the pool to make sure that nothing was needed. Kelsey couldn't imagine what would be. A hot lunch, prepared by Margaret, was waiting for them when they left the pool. It would be served in Bob's house, having been carried across the property by a staff member, so no one would get cold traveling the two minutes to Lisa's house. There was also a large towel warmer, with hanging terry-cloth robes, and stacks of towels steps from the pool, and ready for use. Kelsey suspected, although she wasn't going to ask, that if she wanted, there would be someone available to carry her out of the pool and put her into one of the warm robes.

Tyler swam up next to her and flipped over on his back. He took her hand in the water as he floated with her. They floated for a few minutes, then Kelsey let go of Tyler's hand, and she swam to the side of the pool.

Tyler joined her. "Having fun?" he asked.

"Sure."

"You've were floating for a while."

"I just felt like floating," Kelsey replied.

"Good enough," Tyler said. "The twins are almost done. Are you ready for lunch?"

"I think I'm still full from breakfast, but I'll join you," Kelsey replied.

"Can I get you a robe?" Tyler asked her. Kelsey couldn't help but smile at his words. She knew that there was someone available to carry her out of the pool, but she had been thinking staff, not husband.

"Only if it's warm," she replied.

That afternoon, Kelsey walked into the kitchen in Lisa's house. Margaret's assistant Katie was there, along with Jennifer, a staff member who had been introduced to her the day before. Tyler stood by the counter, drinking a cup of coffee. Kelsey walked over, and with a wink, she took it from him, and began to drink from the cup.

Tyler laughed. "Do you want one?" he asked.

"I have one," Kelsey replied with a giggle. She took another sip.

"Fine, I drink too much coffee anyway. How was your massage?"

"It was great," Kelsey said. She had chosen to have the masseuse use bergamot oil instead of her usual lavender, so she would be alert and awake for the rest of the day.

"Ryan wants to know if we can babysit the twins tomorrow."

"That would be fun," Kelsey said.

"I'll let Ryan know."

"Will we stay at their house?" Kelsey asked.

"Ryan said we can take them out if we want to. He said it helps if Allie gets fussy," Tyler replied.

Kelsey felt a little nervous. "Do you think that we should take them out by ourselves?" she asked. Babysitting at home was one thing, but she wasn't confident about being out in public with them.

"We won't be alone. Aiden will come with us."

"Right, the baby entourage," Kelsey said.

"It may seem lonely, but you're never alone," Tyler replied.

The next morning, Kelsey found herself at Target, Allie sleeping cozily in the baby carrier strapped around Kelsey's body. Ryan had asked them to come over early, so he could surprise Jessica with breakfast in bed. Kelsey supposed that having breakfast delivered to the bedroom wasn't the norm in the Perkins home.

Seconds after Ryan and Jess left for a day of Christmas shopping, Allie started to cry, so Kelsey and Tyler decided to go out right away. Even though it was the last Sunday before Christmas, it was surprisingly quiet in the store, but Kelsey knew it wouldn't be for long.

Tyler, Rory, and Aiden had walked over to the toy department, while Kelsey gently walked with Allie through the cosmetics department. Kelsey noticed the prices. They seemed very cheap compared to what she was used to paying for makeup now. But Kelsey marveled at the fact that it hadn't been that long since she too had bought makeup at Target. Things had certainly changed.

Kelsey wandered toward the toy department, her eyes open for Tyler. But when she spotted him, her eyes got just a little bit wider.

Tyler was standing in the aisle, talking to a woman. A gorgeous woman. She was cooing at Rory, and Rory was holding her finger with his hand.

"Hi," Kelsey said possessively, walking up to them. The woman looked a little startled to see her.

"This is my wife," Tyler said to the woman.

"It's nice to meet you," the woman said to Kelsey. "Bye, Rory," she said, and she turned and left.

"Making friends?" she asked Tyler with mock jealousy.

"It was Rory's idea," Tyler replied. Rory gurgled happily at the sound of his name.

"I'll talk to you later, young man," Kelsey said to Rory, as she gave his tiny foot a gentle squeeze. "Where's Aiden?"

"He said he'd be back," Tyler said. "Are you ready to go?"

"No, it's fine. Allie's sound asleep, and I don't want her to wake up by putting her in the car seat. It looks like I need to keep an eye on the two of you, though."

"Talk to Rory. I'm innocent."

"That I doubt," Kelsey said, taking his hand. Tyler lifted her hand and kissed it. They started to walk.

"So what would you like for Christmas?" Tyler asked.

"Starting your Christmas shopping a little late?" Kelsey teased.

"Everyone knows that you get the best deals close to Christmas Day," Tyler replied.

"And we all know how much Tyler Olsen likes a bargain."

"Exactly. What do you want?"

"Does it have to be from Target?"

Tyler laughed. "No," he said.

"Have you really not bought me a Christmas gift?" From their previous conversation, Kelsey had assumed that he had.

"You seem upset."

"Not upset, surprised. Jeffrey's not here to get it for you."

"Actually, I have already bought a present for you. But I was wondering if there was something that you were wanting."

"No, Mr. Olsen," Kelsey said, looking at Tyler blissfully. "I have everything I want."

"If you want to meet Lucinda Faber, she's at Bob's house," Margaret said to them hours later. They had dropped the twins back off into their parents' loving arms, and had returned to Lisa's house to eat an early dinner.

"Lucinda Faber? Academy-Award-winning actress, Lucinda Faber?" Tyler asked.

"That's the one. Although I don't think she's at Bob's house showing him her Oscar," Margaret quipped.

"She's probably showing him something, but I'd rather not think about what," Lisa said.

"Why don't you stop him?" Tyler asked Lisa. "He listens to you."

"Not about women," Lisa said. "All I can do is remind him to sign prenups and non-disclosure agreements and let him get on with being a teenager."

"Ryan must not know. He didn't mention it," Tyler said to Kelsey.

"He'll find out soon enough," Lisa said. "How were the twins?"

"We had a good time," Tyler said. Kelsey yawned. It had been fun, but watching the twins had worn her out.

"Tired, Kelsey?" Lisa asked her.

"A little."

"I'll have to tell Allie and Rory to be easier on you if I want grandchildren," Lisa commented.

"Are you eating with us or going back to work?" Tyler asked, sitting next to his mother at the counter.

"It's Sunday, I'll work at home."

"Are you going in tomorrow? It's Christmas Eve," Margaret said, as she turned back to the stove.

"I might stay home," Lisa replied. "The office is closed anyway. Are you enjoying your time away from the office, Kelsey?"

"It's been nice," Kelsey said.

"And we still have over a week to go," Tyler said happily.

"Plenty of time to work on the fourth-quarter report," Lisa quipped.

Kelsey walked back into their bedroom a little while later, looking for her Darrow sweatshirt. She was a little cold, and Tyler had offered to turn up the heat, but Kelsey had decided to get something warm to wear instead. Although she didn't have to worry about paying the electric bill now that she was married to a billionaire, she still found that her old habits remained.

As she picked up the sweatshirt from a chair, she heard voices coming from the bathroom, and realized that it was being cleaned by the staff.

"Not a speck of dirt, not a strand of hair," Kelsey heard someone say. "We don't want any problems with Mrs. Olsen."

Kelsey frowned, because she was Mrs. Olsen, and she wondered exactly what problems they were expecting. Mariel cleaned Kelsey and Tyler's

Seattle home, and Kelsey had never had anything but praise for Mariel's work. Confused, Kelsey took the sweatshirt and left the room.

"Oops, sorry," Kelsey said an hour later. She had walked into the family room, where Lisa was sitting on the floor, a Tactec computer in front of her. Kelsey surveyed her mother-in-law with interest. Lisa was dressed more casually than Kelsey had ever seen her. Lisa was wearing a bright pink University of Michigan sweatshirt, black leggings, and her long dark hair was in a ponytail high on her head. It was tied with a silver elastic band.

"I was looking for Tyler," Kelsey said. He had gone to talk to Lisa about work a few minutes earlier, and had asked Kelsey to interrupt them if Zach called. He had, so Kelsey had come downstairs to tell Tyler.

"He'll be right back. Come, sit down," Lisa said graciously, gesturing at the sofa. Kelsey sat. "We were just talking about next quarter. Here he is," Lisa said as Tyler walked in behind the sofa.

Kelsey turned to him and held out his phone. "Zach just called," she said.

"Thanks, Kels," Tyler said, taking the phone. He left the room.

"You and Tyler have had a very busy few months. How are you holding up?" Lisa asked.

"I'm fine," Kelsey replied.

"Tyler says that you're a real trooper," Lisa commented. "Nothing gets you down."

Kelsey laughed. "I'm not sure that's true."

"Well, you survived dealing with my ex-husband, so that's an achievement," Lisa replied with a smile. She looked past Kelsey. "How's Zach?" she asked as Tyler walked back into the room.

"He's fine. He'll be over tomorrow," Tyler said, sitting next to Kelsey and reaching out for a bowl of miniature candy canes. Kelsey had seen him eat about a dozen of them over the past few days, as they were in every room. She watched curiously as Tyler broke off the top of the cane, then broke the long stem in two. Next he opened the plastic package, and starting with the top, ate the candy cane. Kelsey had seen him eat each candy cane in exactly the same way. "Sorry, where were we?" he asked his mother.

"You were explaining to me why three dozen analysts are wrong and you're right about this tiny startup in Orlando," Lisa said.

"Look, I know that the numbers aren't quite there, but they've got a valuable niche and I think that they are just going to get stronger over time."

"So now's the time to buy them?"

"Someone's going to see what I do, and we'll miss our chance," Tyler replied.

"No one's going to see what you do, because the numbers aren't there," Lisa said. "So there's no hurry."

"Lisa, if they look for another round of funding, that's just going to be more people we need to buy out."

"Why don't we just invest?" Lisa asked.

"Because if we acquire them, we can start steering their research in the direction that we want them to go. There's a bunch of very smart engineers there, and the product is still young, so why wait?" Tyler asked her.

"Because I don't want to spend the money," Lisa replied.

"You don't want to spend the money now, and you're going to want to spend a lot more for them later? I don't think so."

"If the price is too high, I won't want to buy them later," Lisa said.

"Oh, yes you will. And it will cost us three times as much," Tyler said firmly.

Lisa twirled the neon pink pen that she held in her hand.

"Convince me," she said to her son.

"What do you want to hear?"

"That I'll see a return after six quarters," Lisa said.

Tyler shook his head. "I can't promise that," he said. "But I can guarantee that you'll see one in three."

"Three quarters? Come on," Lisa said in disbelief.

"I'll bet you. Lisa, these guys are hungry, and they're dying for someone to see the benefit of what they've developed. Tactec buys them, and they are going to want to prove to you that the investment was worth it. "

"Suppose you're wrong?"

"I won't be," Tyler replied.

Lisa twirled the pen in her hand again. She was clearly thinking about Tyler's words.

"OK," She finally said. "No more than two million."

"We can get it for one point six," Tyler said confidently.

"So whose budget should I take it out of?" Lisa asked him, her brown eyes sparkling.

"Not mine," Tyler replied.

"You have a budget at Tactec?" Kelsey asked Tyler later over dessert. They had eaten dinner with Lisa, and she had gone back to her work.

"According to next year's budget I do," Tyler replied, offering her a bite of ice cream. Kelsey ate it.

"So what are you doing next year?" Kelsey asked curiously. Tyler hadn't told her.

"No idea."

"But you have a budget?"

"Yes. But not a title," Tyler said, taking a bite of brownie.

"How is that possible?" Kelsey asked.

Tyler shrugged. "Lisa put the money into second quarter, so I figure she'll have to tell me by then."

"I wouldn't bet on it," Kelsey said. Tyler had been working for Tactec for months, but he still didn't have a specific role. Working in Bob's office was the closest thing he had had to stability at the company.

"Yeah, me neither," Tyler said, offering Kelsey another bite of dessert.

Athena, who's in the house?" Tyler asked as they walked into the foyer of Lisa's house on Monday morning. It was Christmas Eve, and they had just returned from Ryan's.

"Lisa, Kelsey, Rohan, Martin, Jennifer, Katie, Cole, and Quinn."

"Quinn's here? Athena, where's Quinn?" Tyler said.

"Quinn is in the kitchen."

"Come on, I'll introduce you," Tyler said, taking Kelsey's hand and leading her toward the kitchen.

"Who's Quinn?" Kelsey said. She hadn't heard the name before.

"Her father lives two doors down from Bob," Tyler said. "We went to high school together."

"She wasn't at the wedding?"

"Quinn lives in London, with her husband and two kids," Tyler said. "She couldn't make it."

"Tyler!" a voice said happily as they walked into the kitchen. Quinn was a tall, skinny redhead. She was wearing jeans, a blue sweater, and a diamond ring the size of a house.

"Hey, Quinn," Tyler said. "This is Kelsey."

"Your new wife. It's nice to meet you," Quinn said with pleasure.

"You too," Kelsey said.

"It was good seeing you, Quinn. Take care," Lisa said, standing to excuse herself.

"Bye, Lisa," Quinn said, and Lisa left the room.

"What are you doing here?" Tyler asked Quinn.

"Visiting the old man. He says the third heart attack's the charm," Quinn said without mirth.

"How is George?"

"As stubborn as ever. I'm trying to get him to move to London, but he won't budge," Quinn said.

Tyler shook his head. "George is never going to move," he commented.

"I know, but I'll keep trying."

"How long are you here for?" Tyler asked her.

"I'm heading to the airport in just a few minutes. I just wanted to drop by to say hi and meet Kelsey on my way out. Have you given her the grand tour yet?" she asked.

"Now you realize that I can't," Tyler said. He had an odd look on his face, but Quinn just laughed.

"You should anyway," Quinn giggled.

"How's London?" Tyler asked, changing the subject.

"It's good."

"Is Pete here?" Tyler asked.

"No, he stayed home with the girls. I just wanted to check on Dad." Quinn glanced at her phone. "I need to get out of here if I'm going to make my plane. I'm sorry we didn't have more time to talk."

"You'll be back to check on George. Stay a little longer next time," Tyler said to her.

"Sounds like a plan," Quinn said. "I'm glad I didn't miss the two of you," she said, picking up her bag.

"It was nice meeting you," Kelsey said to her.

"Have a good flight, Quinn," Tyler said.

"Welcome to the neighborhood, Kelsey," Quinn said, and she left.

"So have you been working?" Zach asked Tyler an hour later. He had just arrived for a short visit, because he was also on his way to the airport to pick up his great-aunt, who was visiting from California.

"Not much. Lisa's been in the office."

"Lucky you," Zach said.

"She's trying to make a good impression on Kelsey," Tyler commented.

"Is it working?" Zach asked Kelsey.

"I guess so," Kelsey said.

"You don't seem confident," Tyler commented.

"I didn't realize she was doing anything different. I haven't spent a lot of time with your mom," Kelsey said to Tyler.

"True. Normally, by this point in the holiday I would have reviewed about fifty pages of documents, so I'm thinking Lisa's giving me a break because you're here."

"Did you finally find something for Lisa?" Zach asked.

"I bought her a antique Native American basket."

"She'll love that. Did Jeffrey find it for you?"

"I found it myself. I didn't like what Jeffrey suggested."

"What did he suggest?" Kelsey asked curiously.

"To skip the gift this year, and give her my blessing to date Simon," Tyler replied.

Zach burst out laughing. "He didn't," Zach said.

"He did. I should fire him."

"You wouldn't survive a day without Jeffrey," Zach said dismissively. "Jeffrey's certainly not afraid of you."

"He thinks that he's safe because I keep sending him to New York to deal with Chris. He's wrong."

"I don't know. That's a lot more time that you would have to deal with Chris if he wasn't there."

"Some days I think it would be worth it," Tyler replied.

"It wouldn't be," Zach said, as Katie walked into the room.

"Can I get you something to drink?" she asked Zach politely.

"Anything," he replied. "Katie, can you bring me a snack too?"

"Of course," Katie said brightly. "Is there anything else?" she asked. Tyler looked at Kelsey.

"No, thank you," Kelsey said.

"Thanks, Katie," Tyler said, and Katie left the room.

"Hungry?" Tyler asked Zach.

"Starving. I thought I could wait until we went out with Nan, but now I don't think I can make it to the airport."

"Did Reina get off OK?" Kelsey asked.

"She did. They're in Yokohama now."

"Why didn't you go? You're going to ask her to marry you anyway," Tyler said.

"Too much pressure. I don't want to deal with Reina's extended family until I give her the ring."

"Zach, are you really getting married?" Kelsey asked.

"I think I am, Mrs. Olsen. Don't give me that look, Tyler."

"I didn't say anything."

"I know what you're thinking," Zach said.

"What?" Tyler asked.

"That this is a bad idea," Zach replied.

"You're right, that is what I'm thinking," Tyler said.

"Look, Ryan's managed to stay married."

"It's a miracle I had to see to believe," Tyler conceded. "But lightning doesn't strike twice."

"What's the difference between him and me?"

"Jess. She's the best thing that's happened to Ryan since he was born. He's not going to take any chances with her."

"I love Reina," Zach said.

"You've loved a lot of women," Tyler replied.

"I'm not sure I want to have this conversation in front of Kelsey. She might think poorly of me," Zach said.

"There's no reason to hide the truth," Tyler said.

"The truth is that I love Reina, and I'm determined to make it work. So I don't need your pessimism."

"Fine. You're a grown man. Do what you want. But I will say I told you so when the time comes," Tyler replied as Katie walked in carrying a tray. She set it on the coffee table in front of Zach.

"Thanks," he said, and Katie walked out. Zach picked up an open-face sandwich. "No, you won't say I told you so, because 50 years and seven months from now, Reina and I will be celebrating our 50th anniversary."

"If you say so," Tyler said skeptically. He picked up a carafe and poured some of the liquid into a mug. "Apple cider, Kels?"

"Thank you," Kelsey said, taking the warm mug. She took a sip. It was spicy and sweet.

"Suppose I had said that to you? That you wouldn't manage to stay married to Kelsey?"

"I don't have your track record," Tyler pointed out.

"You don't have any track record. You never let anyone get close before Miss North."

"All the more reason I knew she was the one," Tyler said, giving Kelsey a smile.

"What do you think, Kelsey?" Zach asked her.

"About what?" Kelsey asked in surprise.

"Should I marry Reina, or continue to be alone?" Zach asked sorrowfully.

Tyler laughed. "You're tampering with the witness."

"That's the future you want me to have. You, Ryan, Brandon all happily married, and I'm the old maid."

"I just don't want you rushing into this because your parents like Reina," Tyler replied.

"I'm not rushing. Kelsey, what do you think?"

"I think it's up to you," Kelsey replied diplomatically.

"Kelsey agrees with me," Tyler said.

"Do you?" Zach pressed.

Kelsey frowned. "I haven't seen you in a long-term relationship, so I don't have an opinion."

"You saw me with Kim," Zach pointed out.

"All the more reason to take this slow," Tyler said. Kelsey had to agree. Kim had caught Zach cheating on her, and Kim had been heartbroken.

"When we get married, I'm committing to her. Reina's not Kim."

"You know what I think," Tyler said, picking up a sandwich of his own. "I'll go along with whatever you want to do, but honestly, I don't think this is your best idea."

"You never like any of my ideas," Zach said with a shrug.

"I think this is a particularly bad one," Tyler replied.

"Whatever. Kelsey, will you help me pick out Reina's ring?"

"Of course," Kelsey said. Like Tyler, Kelsey was Zach's friend and she would do what he asked her to do. But like her husband, she had her doubts about Zach's ability to stay married.

Zach picked up another sandwich and stood up. "We'll do it soon. I gotta go pick up Nan."

"Tell her we said hi," Tyler said.

"Will do. See you later," Zach said, and he left the room.

Tyler licked cream cheese off the side of the sandwich.

"You're really worried, aren't you?" Kelsey asked.

"This isn't going to end well. Reina's going to get hurt, Zach's parents are going to be angry, and he won't have learned anything."

"Are you sure? Maybe Zach's right. People do change."

"To change you have to learn from your mistakes. I'm not confident that Zach thinks he's made any."

"Not even with Kim?"

"He was going to break up with her anyway. He thinks that getting caught with someone else was just an oversight." Tyler took a bite of his sandwich and chewed slowly. Once he swallowed, he said, "It doesn't matter, we'll do what we have to do, and watch it play out."

"Maybe you'll be wrong," Kelsey said, taking a sip of her cider.

But Tyler shook his head. "I won't be," he replied.

Christmas Eve at the Olsen home seemed quiet to Kelsey in contrast to her parents' home. In Port Townsend, Kelsey would have been helping customers with last-minute gifts and counting the minutes to when she and her parents would finally go home, collapse on the sofa, and eat a frozen pizza.

But on this Christmas Eve, Kelsey was doing none of those things. She and Tyler watched a movie together, lay in bed talking for a while and, finally, watched a beautiful sunset together.

Lisa Olsen arrived home at 8 p.m. She had changed her mind and decided to work at the office on Christmas Eve. She walked into the living room where Tyler and Kelsey were playing Monopoly, and sat in one of the armchairs.

"How was your day?" she asked the couple, as she moved a red sequined pillow from behind her back and tossed it onto the sofa.

"Good. We just hung around," Tyler replied. "How about you?"

"It was fine," Lisa said. "Should we open a present tonight?" she asked.

"Sure," Tyler replied.

Lisa stood up. "I'll go change," she said, leaving the room.

"Do you usually open gifts the night before Christmas?" Kelsey asked.

"Just one," Tyler replied. "We'll open the rest tomorrow morning."

"So Lisa usually doesn't have anything to open on Christmas Day?"

"What do you mean?"

"There's only the two of you, so I would assume that if she opens your gift, there's nothing else for her."

"Bob usually sends something over, and when we lived here, Ryan came over to open gifts with us. There's always a few things under the tree."

"Ryan came over for Christmas, but not Bob?"

"Bob always works on Christmas Day," Tyler replied, standing up. "I need to get something for Lisa. I'll be right back."

"OK," Kelsey said.

"Sorry," Tyler said. He knelt down and gave her a kiss. "Now I can go." Kelsey beamed as he left the room.

Tyler and Lisa returned together a few minutes later. Kelsey had moved the game aside, and was sitting on the sofa as they returned. Tyler sat next to her, and placed a small brown paper tote bag on the coffee table. Then he reached into the bowl of miniature candy canes.

"Want one?" he asked Kelsey. She shook her head, and as usual, Tyler broke off the top of the candy cane, then broke the stem.

"Kelsey, I'd like to give you a gift first," Lisa said, handing Kelsey a beautifully-wrapped box.

"Thank you," Kelsey said, taking it. As Tyler and Lisa watched, Kelsey unwrapped the box and opened it. Inside was a deep blue silk wrap, with gold accents. "Lisa, it's beautiful," Kelsey said.

"It's from Nepal," Lisa said as Kelsey unfolded it and wrapped it around her own shoulders.

"Thank you, Lisa," Kelsey said.

"You're welcome. Tyler, what's in the bag?"

"It's a gift for me, so you should open one," Tyler replied.

"OK," Lisa said. She reached out to one of the side tables and pulled out a box. Kelsey had noticed all of the boxes piled on the side tables but she had assumed that they were for decoration. Clearly she was wrong. Lisa glanced at the card and unwrapped the small box. She pulled out a pair of dangling blue gemstone earrings.

Lisa handed the earrings to Kelsey, who took them to get a closer look. They were stunning as they sparkled in the light of the room. As Kelsey held them out to hand them back, Lisa said, "Keep them."

"They're yours," Kelsey protested.

"They are from a supplier, and I don't wear a lot of blue. They'll go nicely with the wrap," Lisa said, putting the gift box to the side.

Kelsey glanced at Tyler, who gave her a gentle nod to let her know that she should accept the earrings.

"Thank you," Kelsey said, looking at the earrings again.

"It's your turn, Tyler." Lisa said. "Who's your gift from? Kelsey?"

"It's from Chris," Tyler said, looking in the bag and pulling out a envelope. "This is for you."

Lisa didn't reach out for the envelope. "If you're serving me with a lawsuit, I'll kill you," she said.

Tyler laughed. "Take it. Chris promised that it wasn't anything bad."

Lisa took the envelope. "It's probably poisoned," she commented wryly as she opened it with her manicured fingers. Tyler pulled a small box out of the tote, and opened it. Nestled inside of some white tissue paper was a carved wooden bird.

Kelsey glanced at Lisa to see if she had noticed Tyler's present from Chris, but Kelsey realized that Lisa was reading the letter that she had pulled out of the envelope. And as she read, a tear fell from Lisa's eye.

Lisa looked up, and caught Kelsey's glance.

"Excuse me," Lisa said, and she left the room, letter in hand.

Tyler pulled the bird out of the box. Kelsey had seen birds much like this one before, back in Chris's gallery. But unlike those, this one was a little less perfect, a bit rougher around the carved edges. Tyler held the tiny sculpture up and looked at it closely.

"It looks like Chris is getting better," he said, and Kelsey heard the hope in his voice.

"How do you know?" Kelsey asked.

"He said he had just finished this one when I got to New York. It's pretty good."

"Tyler, that's great," Kelsey said. She understood Tyler's hope. When she had last seen Chris he could barely hold a pen, and there was concern about whether he would be able to resume his artistic career. This little bird was a sign that Chris had made great strides in his recovery.

"Where did Lisa go?" Tyler asked, setting the bird down on the table.

"I don't know," Kelsey said. "She was crying when she left."

"Crying?" Tyler said, perplexed.

"I wonder what was in the letter," Kelsey said.

Lisa didn't return, and Tyler suggested that they give her some privacy to deal with whatever Chris had written, so Kelsey and Tyler put their gifts aside and resumed the game. As Tyler was buying his fifth hotel, Kelsey gave him a quick kiss and stood up.

"Do you want something to drink?" she asked him. Looking at the board, and Tyler's many hotels to her three houses, it was clear that — as was usual when playing Monopoly with Tyler — Kelsey could look forward to a quick and expensive loss.

"I'm OK, thank you," Tyler said, reaching for a candy cane. Kelsey brushed his brown hair with her hand and headed for the kitchen. It was dark, but the lights turned on as she arrived. Just as she was about to open a cabinet for a glass, she heard someone say,

"Can I get something for you, Mrs. Olsen?"

Kelsey turned around, and Jason, the house manager, gave her a pleasant nod.

"I was just going to get some water, but I can get it myself," Kelsey said.

"There's no need, I'll bring some for you," Jason replied. "Please go back to what you were doing."

Kelsey wanted to protest, because she was literally one arm's length from a glass, but she sensed that she should not.

"Thank you," Kelsey said, and she left the kitchen.

"So do I get an early Christmas gift?" Tyler asked Kelsey as they walked into their bedroom. Lisa hadn't returned, so they had decided to go to bed, and see her in the morning.

"What would you like?" Kelsey teased as Tyler closed and locked the door behind them.

"You know what I like," Tyler said huskily.

"Well, I don't know. You never let me win at Monopoly," Kelsey said.

"We'll play a different game," Tyler said as he took her into his arms.

Christmas morning was bright and clear, and Kelsey woke up in Tyler's arms.

"Merry Christmas," Kelsey said happily.

"Merry Christmas, Princess," Tyler replied, kissing her. "Thank you for my present."

"I haven't given you a present yet."

"Waking up next to you is the best present of all," Tyler said. Kelsey snuggled next to him and gave him a kiss.

She thought back to where she was this time a year ago. Waking up in her parents' house, riding in Morgan's new Corvette, wishing that she understood what Tyler was doing in his battle with Lisa. Now everything had changed. She was waking up in her new mother-in-law's house, Morgan had moved on from Bob — and the battle, at least about Kelsey, was over. So much was different, yet only 365 days had passed.

Kelsey tapped her wedding ring against Tyler's, and the rings made a soft sound. Tyler lifted Kelsey's hand and kissed it. He looked into her eyes with his own, then he hugged her tightly.

"I'm so happy to have my beautiful wife here with me," he said.

"Thank you for inviting me. It's been really nice," Kelsey said. She had been worried, but of course, Tyler had been right about what life was like in Medina. They had barely seen Lisa, and when they had, she had been gracious and welcoming. Despite their very rocky start, Kelsey had to admit that Lisa was turning out to be a kind mother-in-law.

"You're not too bored?"

"I'm not bored at all. My husband keeps things exciting."

"I could excite you now," Tyler said, kissing Kelsey.

"I'm sure you could. But I want to see my present."

"You are bored," Tyler pouted. "You'd rather see your present than sleep with me."

Kelsey giggled. "Seeing the gift takes thirty seconds. Being in bed with you takes hours. Anyway, you know how impatient I am. Give me my present."

"Maybe I didn't buy one for you," Tyler said petulantly.

"Stop teasing. You said you did."

"I want my Kelsey time now. Gifts later," Tyler said.

"Gimme."

"No."

"Fine," Kelsey said, getting out of bed and wrapping her silk robe around her body. "I'll get it myself."

"Fine," Tyler said, brown eyes sparkling in amusement.

Kelsey looked around the room, but realized that everything had been neatly put away. She glanced at Tyler, who gave her a grin.

"Looking for something?" he asked.

"My gift," Kelsey said sassily. "Maybe it's in the closet," she said, walking to the large walk-in closet, and opening the doors.

"It's not," Tyler called helpfully from the bed.

Kelsey glanced around the closet. If it was here, she would never find it. Tyler's closet was perfectly organized, much like their shared closet at home, and nothing stood out. Kelsey left the closet and closed the doors behind her.

"If you would just give me my gift, I would come back to bed."

"Maybe your gift is in bed," Tyler said suggestively.

"I know what's in bed waiting for me, thank you very much," Kelsey replied.

"Do you?" Tyler asked her. He slipped his hand down next to the side of the bed, and pulled out a beautifully wrapped box.

Kelsey jumped with excitement and ran over to the bed. Tyler puckered his lips and she kissed them.

"Can I have it?" Kelsey asked.

"No," Tyler said, undoing the silk belt around her waist with his free hand. Kelsey's robe fell open. She was wearing nothing underneath.

Kelsey didn't care. At this point, she was so curious she thought she would explode. It wasn't about the gift, it was about her inability to get what she wanted.

So she leaped on Tyler.

Surprised by the sudden movement, Tyler dropped the box back onto the floor. As Kelsey scrambled to retrieve the box, Tyler grabbed her by the waist to pull her away from it. Kelsey laughed in delight as she tried to both remove herself from Tyler's grip and get the box at the same time.

They gently wrestled for a moment, then Kelsey extracted herself just enough from Tyler's hands to reach the box on the floor.

"Got it!" she said in triumph, and clutching the box to herself, she allowed Tyler to pull her back up on the bed.

Kelsey breathed deeply. She was flushed and hot from rolling around with her naked husband on the bed. The robe had slipped off her shoulders, and Kelsey saw the look of desire in her husband's eyes. Holding the hard-won box, Kelsey straddled Tyler with her bare legs.

With a swift movement, Kelsey tossed the box behind her.

"I'll open it later," she said, leaning down to kiss him.

"I'm glad it wasn't fragile." Kelsey said a while later, turning the pages of her Christmas gift from Tyler. He had bought her a book of love poems.

"Don't worry, I knew who I was buying a gift for," Tyler commented, brushing a strand of her hair away from her face. Kelsey's gift to Tyler, a pair of gold cufflinks engraved with their wedding date, sat on the nightstand.

"Your loving wife," Kelsey said, stroking his face. The stubble brushed against her palm.

"Exactly," Tyler said, hugging her and kissing her hair.

After a cuddle, Tyler and Kelsey put on their pajamas and headed down to the living room. Lisa Olsen sat there, typing on her computer, a red Santa hat on her head.

"Merry Christmas," Lisa said brightly.

"Merry Christmas, Mom," Tyler replied.

"Merry Christmas, Lisa," Kelsey added.

"Just give me one second," Lisa said, as she typed. Kelsey was curious as to who was in the office today, but then remembered that Tactec was an international company, and not everyone celebrated Christmas.

"Thanking one of our suppliers in Kuala Lumpur," Lisa said, putting the computer to the side. As she did so, her phone beeped. "Hang on, it's Bob," she said, picking it up.

Tyler glanced at Kelsey, and she gave him a smile.

Two emails and a phone call later, Lisa was ready to open presents. Kelsey was amazed at the number and variety. Tyler had once told Kelsey that Lisa received gifts from Tactec suppliers. It turned out that not only were the gifts screened, opened, and recorded by Camille — so they could be acknowledged with thank-you notes — but also some of the nicest and most interesting gifts actually ended up under the Olsen Christmas tree.

In addition to the earrings that Lisa had re-gifted to Kelsey the night before, this year's gifts included a beautiful matcha tea set, an enormous art book, and a pair of the boldest shoes Kelsey had ever seen. They were cherry-red heels, with ropes of woven leather that tied at the ankle. Lisa looked at them with a critical eye.

"I'm flattered that they think my feet are so small," she said, amused. She picked up her phone and took a picture of them. "See if they fit, Kelsey," Lisa said, handing her the box. "I'll have Camille get me a pair in my size."

Kelsey took the box and tried the shoe on her bare foot. It fit like a dream.

"Perfect. We have our Cinderella," Lisa said, as she unwrapped one of the pineapple cakes that were regularly sent from the Tactec Taiwan office.

Kelsey smiled at Tyler. She knew that she had her prince.

Lisa stood up and brushed some crumbs from her pajama pants. "Come outside," she said. "I have a gift for you."

Tyler and Kelsey looked at each other, stood up and followed Lisa to the front door. She opened it with one hand, balancing her half-eaten pineapple cake in the other. A brand new Tesla sat outside.

"Thanks, Lisa," Tyler said.

"Now you can stop driving a rental," Lisa said, taking a bite of cake.

At the Olsen house, it turned out that there were so many presents that there was no system for opening them. Tyler and Lisa just dove right in. In fact, it didn't matter whose name was on the card, because a lot of the gifts were from suppliers and family friends — so at a certain point, it was just about someone taking off the wrapping paper to see what was underneath.

As an extra pair of hands, Kelsey was tasked with opening presents as well. She opened boxes from the Philippines, Tanzania, and Malta. And just like with the shoes, Lisa was a generous giver. When a box was opened, Lisa usually offered the gift to Kelsey to take.

"Have one, Kels, these are really good." Tyler said, holding out a box that held chocolate-covered cookies.

"*Alfajores*?" Lisa asked him.

"Of course. Joaquin sends them every year," Tyler said as Kelsey took a cookie. "Camille knows I like them."

Kelsey bit into the cookie. It was filled with *dulce de leche*.

"Good, right?" Tyler asked.

"Delicious," Kelsey replied, taking another bite.

"Here," Lisa said, handing a book to Tyler. "I'm sure that you will like this."

"Thanks, Lisa," Tyler said. He held the book out for Kelsey to see. It was a coffee-table book from the Uffizi Gallery in Florence. Kelsey beamed at the memory from her honeymoon. "Is Lorenzo still trying to butter you up?" Tyler asked Lisa.

"If I hear one more time how perfect Rome is for our new European head office, I'm going to cry," Lisa said. Kelsey glanced at Tyler. Lisa's words reminded her of Chris's letter, and from the look on Tyler's face, he was reminded as well.

"When are you going to make a decision?" Tyler asked.

"I haven't decided."

"Why not?"

"I'm not that convinced that it's important. It's not like London is shutting down. I might leave the head office there for now."

"Really?" Tyler said.

"Here's the thing. If I choose to move the head office to another European capital, everyone who isn't chosen is going to be upset. If I do nothing, then everyone will assume that I haven't made a decision yet."

"But what about the staff?" Tyler asked.

"We'll just get working visas for them. It's not a big deal," Lisa replied.

"It's going to be a hassle for HR."

"I don't work for HR," Lisa said.

"It's not even one of your departments. What does Bob say?"

"Naturally, he wants me to make a choice. We'll see. Plenty of time."

Tyler laughed. "Plenty of time for you. Not so much time for everyone else who's going to be affected."

Lisa shrugged. "Not my problem. Hand me a *alfajor*."

Tyler handed his mother one of the cookies. She took a bite and chewed.

"If this isn't one of your problems, what is?" Tyler asked.

"You're a problem," Lisa commented.

"Come on, I'm Mr. Personality. Everyone likes me."

"They're warming to you," Lisa agreed. She handed Tyler a box. "Open this one."

Tyler looked at the tag.

"Beckindale?" he asked his mother. Kelsey looked at the box in Tyler's hands. A gift from one of the richest men in the world.

"Open it," Lisa said. She didn't sound happy.

Tyler removed the luxurious wrapping. He pulled out a large square navy-blue jewelry box, and opened it. An exquisite diamond necklace sat inside the box. Lisa held out her hand, and Tyler gave her the open box.

"Another problem," Lisa said, snapping the box shut.

"Did you have a nice Christmas, Princess?" Tyler asked Kelsey. The presents had been opened, breakfast had been eaten, and the gift wrap and boxes had been recycled.

"I did. I'm guessing that you did too."

"Good guess," Tyler said, kissing her naked chest. Kelsey giggled, and Tyler pulled her closer.

"Did you like your car?"

"I do. That was a surprise. Jeffrey must have told Lisa I wanted one."

"Now what are you going to spend your money on?" Kelsey asked.

"You," Tyler replied.

"No you aren't. I don't need anything else."

"Nothing?" Tyler asked, kissing her again.

"Nothing that you can pay for," Kelsey corrected.

"I'll leave it in the bank. I'm sure Ben will have another dumb idea he'll want me to invest in."

Kelsey laughed. "You don't have to invest in Ben's projects. I won't mind."

"I know," Tyler said, stroking her hair.

"Penny for your thoughts."

"I wasn't thinking about Ben," Tyler said.

"I'll still give you a penny," Kelsey said.

"I want to know what was in Chris's letter." Tyler said. "But I don't want to ask Lisa."

"You could ask Chris. You're going to call him later," Kelsey said.

In fact, she needed to call home too, but she was dreading it, because there was something she needed to discuss with her mother. Something Kelsey needed to hear.

"I already asked. He wouldn't tell me. He just asked me to give it to her, and said that she wouldn't be upset."

"But she was upset," Kelsey pointed out.

"That's a mystery," Tyler mused. "I don't know, maybe I'll ask Lisa about it later. We're here for a couple more days, then we're heading north."

"I can't wait to go back to Vancouver," Kelsey said happily.

"We'll have to wear clothes in the house this time."

Kelsey giggled. Ryan had suggested staying in the beach house where they had spent their honeymoon.

"If our bedroom is far from theirs, I'll make sure I don't wear clothes in our room."

"Done, not a problem," Tyler said briskly. "They can stay in the backyard."

"Tyler," Kelsey scolded.

"There's a small cottage back there. It's really nice."

"They can sleep in the house. Just maybe on a different floor."

"We'll see," Tyler said, nuzzling her and holding her tight.

"OK," Kelsey said blissfully. Lisa had left to join Bob at work, as they were putting the finishing touches on next year's budget. Allie and Rory were taking a nap after their first Christmas, so Kelsey and Tyler would visit the Perkins family later. There was nothing to do, and nowhere to be, but in each other's arms.

Kelsey and Tyler walked over to the Perkins home in the afternoon. The breeze off Lake Washington was cold, but Kelsey felt warm holding her husband's hand.

Ryan opened the door for them, and as they walked inside, they could hear the sound of crying.

"Merry Christmas," Ryan said.

"It seems like it," Tyler said, as he shrugged off his jacket.

"It's fine. Allie doesn't like holidays," Ryan said.

Tyler laughed. "She doesn't like holidays?'

"I think they are a little too exciting for her," Ryan said, taking a bag from Tyler's hand. "Is this for us?"

"Yes, Merry Christmas," Tyler said.

"Thanks, bro," Ryan said. He led the way into the house. Once again, Kelsey looked at the beautiful Christmas decorations.

"Merry Christmas," Jessica said as they walked into the living room. She was dancing with a teary Allie.

"Merry Christmas," Kelsey said. "How's my Allie?" she asked the baby.

"Crabby," Jessica said. "Want to hold her?"

"Of course," Kelsey said. She took off her jacket and held out her arms. Allie wailed.

"Oh, come on," Jessica said to Allie. She started to dance with the baby again. Kelsey giggled.

"Maybe we'll just open gifts," Tyler commented.

"Ryan, you should open something," Jessica said. "He hasn't opened anything all day."

"I'll open Tyler and Kelsey's gift," Ryan said. He opened the bag that Tyler had carried over. "There's a bunch of things in here," he said.

"There's four of you now," Tyler replied.

"Okay, Rory, let's open your gift," Ryan said, taking a small box out of the bag and walking over to Rory, who was sitting quietly in a bouncy seat. Ryan sat on the floor next to the baby and opened the package.

"So cute!" Jessica said as Ryan pulled out a crocheted rattle shaped like a donut. Ryan shook it in front of Rory, who looked at it curiously with his big eyes.

"Open Allie's," Jessica said to Ryan. "Are you ready to see Kelsey yet?" She asked Allie.

"Come on, Allie," Kelsey said, reaching out for Allie. This time, Allie allowed Kelsey to pick her up, and Kelsey began to sway with her.

"Now you can open Allie's gift," Ryan said, holding the gift out to Jessica. Jessica took it and sat on the sofa. She pulled out a floppy stuffed dog.

"Adorable!" Jessica said. "Allie, look," she said, but Allie was busy putting her hands in Kelsey's hair. "Well, I like it. Thank you," she said. "Open yours, Ryan."

Ryan pulled out a thin box and looked inside of it. Then he burst out laughing.

"Thanks a lot, Tyler," he said with sarcasm. Jessica and Kelsey looked at each other. Kelsey didn't know what Tyler had got for Ryan, but a moment later, Ryan held up a brand new Tactec tablet.

"It's got two 20 megapixel cameras. Perfect for taking selfies with the babies," Tyler said, with a wink to Kelsey. She and Jessica started laughing.

"The perfect gift," Jessica said between giggles.

"That Tyler took out of a storeroom at Tactec," Ryan commented.

"I'll have you know that I had to go to three storerooms before I could find one," Tyler replied.

"I'm touched by your efforts," Ryan said with a grin.

"Now I'm worried about my gift," Jessica said, pulling it out of the bag.

"Don't be, Kelsey bought it for you," Tyler said.

"Then I know it will be good," Jessica said brightly. She took the wrapping off the box. Jessica opened the box and looked inside. "Oh, Kels," she said, pulling out a stunning black bag with rose gold accents. Jessica hugged the bag. "I couldn't find one anywhere. How did you get it?"

"Morgan worked on the designer's birthday party a few months ago," Kelsey said. "When I told Morgan that you were looking for the purse, she reached out to the designer, and he offered to make one especially for you."

Jessica looked teary-eyed. "You're the best friend ever. Please thank Morgan for me."

"I will," Kelsey said, bouncing Allie.

"Time to post on Insta," Jessica said.

"Want to borrow my new tablet?" Ryan asked, laughing.

"I'll pass, thanks," Jessica said, pulling out her own phone. "Ryan, take Allie, so Kelsey can open her present."

Kelsey gave Allie an extra cuddle before handing her to Ryan. Ryan's blue eyes shined as he took his baby daughter.

"It's the green box under the tree," Jessica said.

Tyler handed Kelsey the box, which was medium-sized, but not heavy. Kelsey sat on the sofa, and opened the box. She smiled as she pulled out the designer bag, that had "Mrs. Olsen" elegantly hand-painted on the side.

Kelsey loved the bag, but wondered if she could wear such a bold statement.

"Everyone knows who you are anyway," Jess said, seemingly reading Kelsey's thoughts as she sat next to Kelsey. "Might as well remind them."

"I like it," Tyler said, his brown eyes sparkling.

"Of course you do," Jessica said.

"So do I. Thanks, Jess," Kelsey said, giving Jessica a hug.

"What did you get for me, Ryan?" Tyler asked him.

"I haven't been to the office lately, so I didn't have time to get you anything. I think there might be some post-it-notes lying around," Ryan replied.

"So funny. Give me my gift," Tyler said.

"It's the gold box under the tree," Jessica said, giggling.

Kelsey watched as Tyler opened it. Seeing the gifts in these two houses had been very interesting to her. There had been a mix of expensive gifts and small tokens, and every one of them seemed to be appreciated — or in Ryan's case, to be a source of amusement.

"Thanks," Tyler grinned. He pulled a navy-blue Darrow sweatshirt out of the box.

"It's the latest model," Ryan commented as he bounced Allie. "I thought about having 'World's greatest law review editor' put on the back, but it was too expensive."

"Well, I'm glad you thought of me," Tyler said, taking off his cashmere sweater and putting on the sweatshirt.

"It fits perfectly," Kelsey giggled.

"Too bad. I mean, great," Ryan teased.

"Thanks, Ryan," Tyler said.

"You're welcome," Ryan replied.

"So have you had a good Christmas?" Jessica asked, picking Rory up and cuddling him.

"It's been really nice," Kelsey said.

"Lisa got a million-dollar necklace from Beckindale."

"Are you kidding me?" Ryan said. "Isn't he still married?"

"I'll look," Jessica said, balancing Rory as she scrolled on her phone. "According to Wikipedia, he is," she said.

"How did Lisa feel about her gift?" Ryan asked.

"She seemed displeased," Kelsey commented.

"Yeah, he's kind of old," Jessica said. The other three looked at her. "What?"

"I think you were supposed to say that she already has a boyfriend, Jess," Ryan answered.

Jess shrugged. "For some women, billions are more important than boyfriend."

"Lisa can't manage to spend the money she has, so that wouldn't get her to dump Bill Simon. Unfortunately," Tyler added.

"You'd rather have Beckindale for a stepfather than Simon?" Ryan asked.

"Beckindale has a nice plane," Tyler replied, giving Kelsey a wink. She glared at him.

"Well, Lisa doesn't seem interested," Kelsey said.

"Uh, oh. Are you rooting for a Olsen/Simon wedding, Kelsey?" Ryan asked.

"Of course not," Tyler said.

"Lisa should date whoever she wants to," Kelsey said firmly.

"And Tyler, what do you think about that?" Jessica asked.

"I think we should change the topic," Tyler replied.

"You're back," Lisa said hours later as Kelsey and Tyler walked in the door. Kelsey was grateful for the warm air that surrounded them in the foyer of the house. It was 6:45 p.m., dark outside, and very cold.

"Were you looking for us?" Tyler asked, unwrapping his scarf from around his neck. It was the one that Kelsey had made for him, years ago, and she was always honored that he still wore it regularly.

"No, I knew you were at Ryan's. I was just wondering when we were going to have dinner," Lisa said innocently. Immediately, Kelsey's warning bells sounded. Lisa Olsen was not innocent.

"What's going on?" Tyler asked her. Kelsey knew that, from his words, his warning bells had gone off too.

Lisa hesitated. "I was wondering about how you would feel about us having a guest at Christmas dinner tonight."

"Who?"

Lisa bit her lip. "Bill," she said.

Tyler sighed. "Really?"

"It's Christmas, Tyler," Lisa said, in her Mom voice, perfectly calibrated to create guilt. Kelsey knew the tone well.

"Fine," Tyler said. Lisa didn't move. "You already invited him, didn't you?" he surmised.

Lisa gave him a guilty smile of her own. "He's on the way."

"Great," Tyler said. "Excuse me." He walked away from his mother and up the stairs. Kelsey gave Lisa a smile and walked after Tyler.

"Why?" Tyler said, as soon as Kelsey closed their bedroom door.

"It's only dinner, Tyler," Kelsey said soothingly. "You've had dinner with Bill before."

"Pizza. At work."

"Pretend we're working."

"Christmas dinner. Easter. Thanksgiving. Am I going to have to deal with Bill Simon every holiday from now on?"

"We won't be here next Christmas," Kelsey said positively.

"You're not helping."

"Sorry," Kelsey said. She gave Tyler a hug.

"It's not your fault. It's mine. They would have never gotten back together if I hadn't worked for him."

Kelsey rubbed the sleeve of Tyler's jacket. "Tyler. It will be fine."

Tyler leaned down and kissed her.

"It better be," he replied.

As Kelsey expected it would, walking into dinner felt a little awkward. Bill arrived promptly at seven, and Kelsey managed to coax Tyler downstairs by 7:10. Kelsey knew exactly when Bill had arrived, because Tyler had told Athena to announce Bill's entrance, and Tyler had pouted for several minutes, until Kelsey got up and dragged Tyler off the bed where they had been lying, fully clothed.

Bill had brought Lisa a Christmas bouquet of red and white roses and they were chatting at the table as Kelsey and Tyler walked into the dining room.

"Merry Christmas," Kelsey said to Bill as Tyler helped her into her chair.

"Same to you," Bill said. Tyler sat next to Kelsey, silently. Lisa looked from Bill to Tyler, then back to Bill, but said nothing. It was clearly going to be a long night.

Katie, who was dressed in a cute red gingham apron, came in with a large plate of carved turkey, and set it on the table.

"Thank you, Katie," Lisa said to her, and Katie walked out.

"Did you have a nice Christmas, Kelsey?" Bill asked her.

"It's been great," she replied.

"How are your parents?" Lisa asked.

"I haven't called them yet," Kelsey commented.

"Have you talked to your kids?" Tyler asked Bill.

Kelsey frowned. Tyler knew, as did Kelsey, that Bill didn't get along with his three adult children.

"Not today," Bill said diplomatically.

"Well, it's been nice having Tyler and Kelsey home," Lisa piped up. "It's been a while."

"Right, because last Christmas Tyler was on the East Coast on vacation, instead of with his mother," Bill said pointedly.

"Yes, well, that was last year. Let's eat," Lisa said hurriedly, as she picked up the serving forks.

Everyone managed to fill their plates without incident. The food was delicious. Although they had eaten a similar menu of turkey and stuffing at Thanksgiving, for Christmas Margaret had made a Scandinavian feast. There were two types of meatballs, one with brown gravy and one with cream sauce, along with smoked salmon, six types of vegetables, and to Kelsey's delight, a small dish of lutefisk, just for her.

"Would you like some?" Kelsey asked Bill.

"No, thank you. I've had the pleasure," he replied.

Lisa laughed. "Oh, I remember that. That was awful," she said.

"That's why your mother doesn't like me," Bill said.

"Is that why?" Tyler piped in.

Kelsey nudged him under the table, but Tyler ignored the warning.

"My grandmother is a very good judge of character," Tyler added. To Kelsey's surprise, Lisa laughed in amusement.

"Well, she doesn't like me either, so I guess that explains that," Lisa said, continuing to laugh.

"I guess I'm in good company," Bill said, and he gave Lisa a smile.

The rest of dinner was uneventful. They avoided the topics of their shared work, and instead discussed their favorite places to go in Vancouver. It turned out that Bill and Lisa had gone to Vancouver many times in the past, because they had spent a few moments discussing whether the tiny motel they used to stay in was still open. After checking on Bill's phone, it turned out that it was.

"Right by English Bay, less than a hundred dollars a night. It was great," Lisa said. "Tyler, you stayed there a couple of times."

"We should go back," Bill said.

"Rohan would never let me stay there," Lisa said. "Remember, the locks barely worked."

"I thought Rohan worked for you."

"Think again. Bob's place is nice. Did you like it, Kelsey?" Lisa asked her.

Kelsey froze. Lisa may have known that Kelsey had stayed at Bob's condo in Vancouver, but it was clear that Lisa didn't know the circumstances of Kelsey's visit, just after her break-up with Tyler.

"It was very nice," Kelsey said, a diplomat in her own right. In fact, Bob's Vancouver condo was still full of tears, the ones that Kelsey had shed because of Lisa. Kelsey brushed the bad feelings aside, and took another bite of lutefisk.

"We should stay there next time," Lisa said to Bill. "You're staying at the beach house when you go, Tyler?" she asked.

"Ryan wants to, but I'd rather stay downtown. The beach is too cold right now."

"Stay at Bob's. He won't be there," Lisa said breezily. Kelsey felt her stomach flip.

"We'll see," Tyler replied, glancing at Kelsey. He knew how Kelsey felt about the condo, and she suspected that he knew it was still too soon for her to stay there. Maybe in a year or two, the bad feelings would be a distant memory, once Kelsey had more good memories with Tyler.

Bill and Lisa skipped dessert so they could walk over to visit the babies before their bedtime. Tyler and Kelsey ate Christmas cake in the family room. Kelsey offered Tyler a bite of the chocolate-and-vanilla cake from her fork, and he ate it.

"I wasn't sure I was going to survive," Tyler commented.

"You did good," Kelsey said.

"So did you. Maybe I should tell Lisa not to mention Bob's condo in front of you."

"It's fine, Tyler," Kelsey said. "Remember, I have a better memory there, thanks to you."

"I do remember," Tyler said. "I like making memories with you," he said, kissing her neck.

Kelsey blushed. "We can make some more later. I need to call home. Will you call Chris?"

"It's late there. I sent him a message and said we'd talk tomorrow."

Kelsey put her fork down on her plate. "Let me call now," she said. "My parents have to fly out early tomorrow."

"OK. Tell them I said hi," Tyler said.

"I will," Kelsey said, picking up her phone and leaving the room.

She walked up the stairs, but instead of returning to their bedroom, she walked into an empty guest room down the hall. Out of the lakeside window, the moon shone on the water, with the bright lights of Seattle beyond. The room illuminated seconds after she stepped inside.

Kelsey looked at her phone and dialed. Normally, she would look forward to a holiday phone call with her parents — but today, Kelsey had something on her mind.

"Merry Christmas," Kelly North said when she picked up the phone.

"Hi, Mom. Merry Christmas," Kelsey replied.

"Should I get your father and put you on speaker?" her mother asked.

"Not yet," Kelsey said. "I wanted to talk to you first."

"Is everything OK?" Kelly North asked.

"Yes. I just had a question," Kelsey paused, then said, "I'm wondering why you didn't talk to me when I was at home."

"What do you mean? We talked," her mother replied.

"You said something to me a couple of times but it's not like we had a conversation. I talked to Mama Jefferson more than I talked to you."

Kelly North was quiet for a moment before she replied. "I guess, Kelsey, I think that you're not really interested in what I'm going to say. So I think that maybe it's better to be quiet."

"I see."

"I love you. I'm glad that you came home for a visit."

Kelsey hesitated before asking the question she had called home to ask.

"Are you proud of me?" Kelsey asked.

"Of course I am," Kelly North said automatically.

"How come?" Kelsey pressed. She wasn't willing to accept a rote answer. This was too important to her.

"A lot of reasons. I think I'm mostly proud that you are a happy, functioning adult."

"Because you didn't expect me to be?"

"No, because it's hard," her mother said, to Kelsey's surprise. "I was really struggling when I was your age. I was married. I had a new baby, and my husband was starting a business. I had no idea how I was going to feed you, never mind myself. I was sure that I was going to fail. But you have made it look effortless. You graduated, got a great job, and have married a good man. And you did every bit of it without my input. So I guess I think that you can handle your own life. I'm not sure that I have a lot more to say."

Kelsey felt a lightness where she hadn't realized there was pain. "Even though I don't always agree with you, I appreciate your concern about me," Kelsey said.

"Always?"

"Always," Kelsey admitted. "You know, Mom, I don't always have it together."

"I know," her mother said, "But you're doing a great job anyway."

"Everyone's fine?" Tyler asked as Kelsey walked back into the family room an hour later. She sat next to him and put her head on his shoulder. Tyler put his arm around her and gave her a kiss.

"Yes. My parents are packing for their cruise, Grandma sent a bunch of pictures of herself with her new shipmates, Jasmine doesn't think that Jace's new girlfriend is good enough for him, Dylan isn't talking to Ian this week, and Morgan is heading out to have Christmas dinner with her new boyfriend," Kelsey said, summing up her many conversations.

"And you? Are you fine too?"

"I am now," Kelsey said, snuggling against Tyler. She glanced up at him. "How about you?"

"I've been better. Bill returned with Lisa, so I think he's planning on staying here tonight. I miss the days when I didn't know who Lisa was dating."

Kelsey looked at Tyler in sympathy. "At least they aren't getting married," she said.

"Soon," Tyler added. "Getting married soon."

Kelsey gave her husband's arm a gentle rub.

"Should we watch a movie?" Tyler asked her. "That will help me get my mind off things."

"That's fine," Kelsey said, "But remember, there's one more gift waiting for you tonight."

Tyler looked at her curiously, then he smiled. "What color is it? Blue?"

Kelsey shook her head. "Black." She stroked his handsome face with her hand. "Lace," she added.

"I think the movie will have to wait," Tyler said.

"You think?"

"I think so," Tyler replied huskily as he rose from the sofa. "I want my present."

Kelsey remained on the sofa.

"It's just a tiny piece of silk. What's the big deal?" Kelsey teased, but as she did so, she felt herself get warm. The thought of Tyler taking that tiny piece of silk off her body made her burn with longing.

"My present isn't the lingerie. My present is you," Tyler replied, holding out his hand. Kelsey took it, and allowed him to pull her up, off the sofa and into his arms. Tyler kissed her, and Kelsey closed her eyes. Her breathing was getting faster.

"Let's go upstairs," Tyler whispered in her ear.

"Only if you have a present for me too," Kelsey replied, kissing him.

On the morning after Christmas, Kelsey and Tyler were sitting in the family room reading when Zach walked in.

"Hey," Tyler said, looking up.

"How's it going?' Zach said, sitting in a soft chair. "Did you get what you wanted for Christmas, Kelsey?"

Kelsey felt herself blush. "I did," she replied. "How about you?"

"I got a new car."

"You too?" Tyler said. "What did you get?"

"Another Land Rover. You?"

"Tesla."

"You've been wanting one. Jeffrey spilled to Lisa?"

"Must have," Tyler replied.

Kelsey watched them in fascination. To Tyler and Zach, cars were run-of-the-mill, everyday Christmas gifts, nothing special. She couldn't imagine ever feeling that way.

"Up for a game of one on one?" Zach asked. "Unless you want to play, Kels."

"I'll watch," she said.

Tyler put his book on the side table and stood up. "Let's go," he said.

Fifteen minutes later, Kelsey sat on the edge of the driveway, bundled up in her warm jacket, as Tyler and Zach ran around, the orange basketball flying around the makeshift court. Kelsey knew that at one of the houses there was an actual, regulation-sized court — but for the purposes of this game, Tyler and Zach seemed content with the basketball hoop that hung over the garage doors.

"Time!" Zach called out. "I need a towel," he explained.

"I'll get one," Kelsey said, scrambling to her feet. Every since she had arrived at the Medina house, she hadn't been able to do much of anything for herself. There were staff members everywhere. Finally, here was an opportunity for Kelsey to be helpful.

"Thanks, Kels," Zach said as Kelsey dashed back to the house. She went inside, and walked into one of the lower-level powder rooms. But she looked around curiously. There wasn't a towel in sight.

Just as Kelsey was about to head to a different powder room, a young woman holding a stack of perfectly-folded towels ran up to her.

"I'm sorry, Mrs. Olsen. I was just about to bring some more towels," she said, very apologetically.

"It's fine. Thank you," Kelsey said. "May I take one?"

"Of course. I'm so sorry," the young woman said. Kelsey took a towel from the pile the woman was holding and, shoulders slumped, the woman walked into the now-empty powder room.

Kelsey felt uncomfortable. It was as if the woman had thought she was going to get into trouble, even though she was doing her job. It was particularly odd to Kelsey because she had seen this same woman before, chatting casually with Lisa. Kelsey thought back to the staff members in her room, and her encounter with Jason last night. Everyone knew that Lisa and Tyler were kind to their staff members.

But at that moment, Kelsey realized that perhaps the staff had a different opinion of her.

"Did I do something wrong with the staff?" Kelsey asked Tyler. They were sitting on the sofa, holding hands and watching the sunset's final rays over Lake Washington.

"Wrong? What do you mean?"

Kelsey sighed. "I don't know. I sense that everyone is tiptoeing around me, like I'm really fussy."

"You are fussy," Tyler laughed.

"I am with you," Kelsey pouted. "Not with the staff."

"That's fair. Come on," Tyler said, pulling Kelsey up. "Let's go ask Margaret." They walked into the kitchen where Margaret was cutting cucumbers. There were a number of ingredients sitting out around her, and Kelsey realized that Margaret was making homemade pickles.

"So Kelsey thinks that the staff is afraid of her," Tyler said to Margaret without preamble.

"Not exactly," Kelsey said, in explanation. "But kind of," she added, unsure of how to continue.

Margaret looked uncomfortable.

"You know something?" Tyler asked.

"Kelsey er her," Margaret said to Tyler in Norwegian.

"Og så?" Tyler replied in Norwegian, shrugging.

"Jeg vil ikke at du skal bli flau," Margaret replied, and despite the fact that Kelsey had no idea what Margaret had said, she thought she detected a note of seriousness in how she said it.

Tyler looked at Margaret curiously.

"Kelsey, can we have a minute?" Tyler asked.

"Of course," Kelsey said.

"Thanks," Margaret said, giving Kelsey a smile. Then she began speaking rapidly in Norwegian. Kelsey watched Tyler as he listened.

"OK," Tyler said to Margaret after a moment. Margaret continued.

"I see," Tyler said a moment later. Margaret began speaking again, and after the next few words, Tyler laughed.

"Really?" he said glancing at Kelsey with a grin on his face. Margaret nodded yes. "All right, thanks. I'll tell Kelsey the details. Tell everyone not to be afraid of her."

"I've told them, but no one's listening," Margaret said in English.

"After what you just said, I guess I can see why," Tyler said. He gave Kelsey a wink. "Come on, I'll give you the scoop on the terrifying Mrs. Olsen." he said, leading her out of the kitchen.

"What did I do? What did Margaret say?" Kelsey asked as they headed back to the living room.

Tyler laughed. "It's actually pretty funny."

"Tyler, it's not," Kelsey said. *What had she done?*

Tyler continued to laugh as they resumed their seats on the sofa. He glanced at Kelsey, took a deep breath, then laughed again.

"Tyler!"

"Ok, fine. Sorry," Tyler said. He was thoughtful. "What should I tell you first?"

"What did Margaret say? Why did she want to tell you in Norwegian?"

"Margaret said that she didn't want me to be embarrassed in front of you," Tyler said, taking Kelsey's hand.

"Embarrassed?" Kelsey said, confused.

"For starters, everyone isn't afraid of you. Katie, Mariel, everyone who knows you is fine with you."

"But?"

Tyler smiled. "Mrs. Olsen has gained a reputation for having things her own way, and at least a few of the staff members are concerned about what that means while you're here."

Kelsey looked at Tyler, a little puzzled. In the meantime, Tyler seemed completely amused.

"Continue," Kelsey said.

"So bossy," Tyler said, laughing again.

Kelsey sighed impatiently.

"Why did we move from Belltown?" Tyler asked her.

"We're playing a game?"

"Just answer the question," Tyler said with a smile.

Kelsey shrugged. "Because I wanted to be closer to work, and my husband is way too nice."

"The staff thinks that you were jealous of Jessica's new house, and you insisted on a big space of your own, and whined at me until I gave in," Tyler said.

Kelsey's mouth dropped open in shock.

Tyler continued. "When we returned from New York, you wouldn't get off Bob's plane, presumably because you were pouting about something. You made Lisa late for her own event because you couldn't decide what to wear. And Jennifer saw you take a cup of coffee directly out of my hands and drink it yourself."

Tyler's brown eyes sparkled in amusement as Kelsey processed his words.

"Is that all?" Kelsey asked.

"I think so. For now," he added, with a grin.

"Unbelievable," Kelsey said, shaking her head.

"Poor Tyler," Tyler said. "I wonder if he knew what his bride was really like," he teased.

"I can't believe they think that about me."

"It doesn't matter. None of it's true," Tyler said, kissing her hand.

"They really think that I made you buy our new home because I was jealous?" Kelsey said.

Tyler looked at her and put his arm around her shoulders. "Don't be upset. It's funny," he said to her.

"It's not," Kelsey said, sniffling. "I'm not like that."

"Of course you aren't. I'm the one who wanted to move into Bob's apartment in New York."

Kelsey frowned. "They think I'm behind that too," she said.

"Sorry, Kels. Look, the staff doesn't have anything better to do than create drama. You're new, so why not create drama about you?"

"So they hate me."

"No, they're just a little worried about upsetting you. They'll get to know you and everything will be fine."

"They've already decided what I'm like, so they probably won't give me a chance."

"Don't worry about it. Margaret, Martin, Jeffrey. Everyone that we have to deal with on a regular basis likes you. It's fine."

"I want everyone to like me."

"Well, see, that's your problem."

"You know what I mean."

Tyler kissed her. "You're so cute when you pout," he said.

"Then the staff must think I'm adorable."

Tyler laughed. "Kelsey, don't let this get to you. Let them think whatever they want. It's like Instagram. People believe what they want to believe, but it has nothing to do with the real you."

"I guess. I just don't want people to think I'm going to yell at them when they see me."

"They'll figure it out."

"I guess so."

"I love you, Mrs. Olsen."

"I love you too, Tyler."

"What will you make me give you next?" he asked, kissing her fingers.

Kelsey felt a tingle up her spine.

"I have some ideas," she replied with a smile.

On Thursday, two days after Christmas, Lisa struck.

"I'm sorry, Kelsey," Tyler said to her.

Kelsey giggled. "Better you than me. When do you think you'll be done reviewing the fourth-quarter report?"

"Three hours?"

"That's fine. I'll see if Jess is up for a visit," she said, giving her husband a kiss.

"She's a Tactec employee. Ask her to come over and help me. Ryan too."

"I won't. They need some family time before we go back to work."

Tyler put his arms around Kelsey's waist. "I need family time too." he reminded her.

Kelsey gave him another kiss. "Later," she said.

"You promise?"

"I do," Kelsey said.

"OK, then you can go. Bring me some vegan snacks back."

"I will," Kelsey said. She gave him one more kiss, then she left the room.

A few minutes later, Kelsey was holding Allie in the Perkins kitchen. Rory was asleep in his mother's arms.

"So Ryan, what are you making?" Kelsey asked as Allie sleepily grabbed Kelsey's long hair.

"Chocolate chip cookies."

"Butter-free, egg-free, milk-chocolate-chip-free cookies." Jessica commented.

"Kind cookies," Ryan countered.

Jessica sighed deeply, and Kelsey giggled.

"I'm sure they'll be delicious," Kelsey said diplomatically. "How have you all been?"

"Great," Ryan said. "It's nice having everyone home."

"Everyone but Bob," Jessica said to Kelsey.

"He's home," Ryan said.

"Barely. When he's not at work, he's holed up in his house with some actress. There have been three since you got to Lisa's," Jessica added.

"Bob doesn't like the holidays," Ryan said. "He always distracts himself."

"Yes, well, I imagine all of those women are quite a distraction," Jess said sarcastically.

"Jess, he's just having fun," Ryan commented.

"He's a grown man. Dating everyone in *Vogue* should be less interesting at that age."'

"Jess," Ryan said.

"Fine, whatever," Jessica said, rocking Rory. "Is she asleep yet?"

"Almost," Kelsey replied, looking down at Allie. "Did you enjoy the rest of Christmas?"

"Allie cried at the Christmas music, refused to eat dinner, and yelled every time Rory tried to play with a toy. So I'm thinking that this is the new normal," Jessica said.

"She's precious," Kelsey said. "Fussy, just like godmother Kelsey."

"Maybe godmother Kelsey wants to babysit again," Jessica teased.

"Any time," Kelsey said, rocking the now-sleeping Allie.

"Are you sure that you aren't ready for parenthood?" Ryan asked.

"Not yet. Tyler and I haven't even reached our first anniversary."

"They have plenty of time, Ryan," Jessica said. "Let me put Rory in the crib, then I'll take Allie," she said, carefully standing, and leaving the room.

"Ryan, Tyler asked me to bring some vegan snacks back for him."

"He asked for vegan snacks?"

"He did."

"Maybe I won't be the only vegan in the houses soon," Ryan said happily.

"Maybe," Kelsey said doubtfully. "Did you have a good Christmas?"

"I did. It's nice having Christmases with Jess, and now we have the babies. My Christmas was perfect."

Kelsey thought Ryan's comment was interesting after their previous conversation about Bob. "What did you get?" Kelsey asked. Ryan hadn't opened his gifts when they had been visiting on Christmas day.

"Jess knit me another sweater. I have no idea how she found time to make it, so it's really special to me," Ryan said. "Bob sent over a check, and Lisa and Bill gave us a weekend away, and said that they would look after the babies."

Kelsey thought that it was interesting that Lisa and Bill gave a joint present, but she was more interested in Ryan's other comment.

"Have you seen Bob lately?" she asked.

Ryan thought for a moment. "No," he replied.

Kelsey thought the answer was curious, but decided not to pry further. According to Tyler, Bob never liked to celebrate Christmas, married or not.

"You could invite him to Vancouver with us," Kelsey said.

"I did, but he said he had a lot of work. Since both Jess and Tyler work for him at Tactec, Bob might want to give them a break. It's OK. Now that I have my new visa, I'm sure we'll start going up again regularly."

"Probably."

"Tyler said that you didn't want to stay in the condo and he doesn't want to stay at the beach house. So I suppose we'll stay at a hotel," Ryan said, walking over to Kelsey with a plate of cookies. "I can take Allie," he said, putting the plate down.

"OK," Kelsey said, giving Ryan's daughter to him. Allie sniffled at the transfer, but fell right back asleep.

Kelsey picked up a warm cookie and bit into it as Ryan rocked Allie.

"I'm going to miss this," Ryan said as he cuddled the baby gently.

"You're working three days a week," Kelsey pointed out.

"I don't need to work at all."

"That's true," Kelsey said.

"Why do you work?" Ryan asked.

"It's good for me," Kelsey replied.

"You think like Bob," Ryan said. "He thinks it's good to work too."

"I know it's good for me. I can't speak for everyone else," Kelsey said as Jess walked back into the room.

"Aw, she's asleep too. Do you want me to put her down?" Jess asked, looking at Allie.

"I'll do it. I only have a few more chances to do this," Ryan commented. "Visit with Kels," he said, and he took Allie out.

"Has Ryan been complaining about working?" Jessica asked, picking up a cookie. "It's like he's going to war."

"He was complaining only a little," Kelsey replied.

"There's going to be a parent with them every single day. It's just not always going to be him." Jessica bit into the cookie and chewed. "Not bad," she commented.

"Yeah, I was expecting them to be terrible, but they're actually great," Kelsey said, taking another cookie.

"I give Ryan a hard time about being vegan, but actually, the food's been really delicious. Don't tell him, though."

"Why not?"

"As long as he suspects I don't love everything that he cooks, he won't nag me about going vegan."

Kelsey giggled, and bit into her cookie. "So how are things at Lisa's?"

"Everything's fine. Zach's been by a couple of times."

"And you met Quinn," Jessica said meaningfully.

"Sure. We told you that when the two of us were here."

"But Tyler was here, so I couldn't ask you about her. How was it meeting her?"

"What do you mean?" Kelsey asked, confused by the tone in Jessica's voice.

"You know who Quinn is, right?" Jess asked.

"Tyler's neighbor," Kelsey replied.

"That's what he told you?"

"She's not?" Kelsey asked, more confused than ever.

Jessica bit her lip. "I've said too much," Jess said.

"Tell me what you know," Kelsey said, but Jess shook her head.

"Ask Tyler," Jess replied.

Jessica refused to say anything more about Quinn the rest of the visit, and Kelsey didn't want to ask in front of Ryan, so Kelsey was quite curious about Jess knew. Kelsey ran her meeting of Quinn through her mind, but nothing stood out. She would have to ask Tyler.

"You're back," Tyler said happily as Kelsey walked in to the living room at Lisa's house.

"Hi," Kelsey said, beaming. She had missed him. Tyler took the computer from his lap, and Kelsey took its place. Tyler burrowed his face into her chest, and Kelsey giggled.

"Tyler," she warned, but she was laughing. She stroked his hair.

Tyler looked at her with his big brown eyes. "I'm almost done, so I can take you to bed," he said.

"It's one in the afternoon," Kelsey replied.

"So?"

"I guess it doesn't matter," Kelsey said.

"No, because we're on vacation."

"At least I am," Kelsey said.

"I will be again."

"Not if Lisa catches up with you."

"She went to the office. I'm safe for now."

"She doesn't have a phone?" Kelsey teased.

"I'm not answering mine," Tyler replied.

"What if she calls the house?" Kelsey asked, removing Tyler's hand from inside her sweater.

"We'll be in our room with the door shut and a 'do not disturb' sign on the doorknob."

"That sounds very nice," Kelsey said, kissing him.

Tyler stroked her hair.

"Jade has arrived," Athena said.

"Jade?" Kelsey said in surprise.

"I thought Jade was in Cartagena," Tyler said.

"Let's go find out," Kelsey said, getting up from Tyler's lap. They two of them walked out and headed to the foyer. Clearly they weren't the only people curious about Jade, because as they reached the front, several staff members were there as well.

"I'm fine," Jade was saying as they walked up. But at least from Kelsey's viewpoint, Jade wasn't. From the moment that she met Jade, Kelsey had always been in awe of her style. The Jade standing at the entryway had a completely different look than Kelsey was used to. Sweats, old sneakers, and her hair in a messy ponytail — the only things that this Jade had in common with the old one were the chic sunglasses over her eyes. Although Kelsey couldn't see Jade's eyes, Jade saw her.

"Kelsey, I'll be back on duty tomorrow," Jade said.

"OK," Kelsey replied. Of course, while Kelsey was staying in Lisa's house, Jade's presence wasn't necessary, but Kelsey assumed that by being on duty, Jade would get back the vacation days that she wasn't using now.

"I'm heading over to the annex," Jade said, waving away offers of help. She hiked her duffel bag over her shoulder, and walked out.

The second the front door closed, everyone was abuzz.

Why had Jade returned early?

Two hours later, the question of Jade's early return had been pushed out of Kelsey's mind. She lay hot and sweaty in Tyler's arms, and she stroked his chest with the tips of her fingers.

"Magic. That's what you are."

"I thought I was your princess."

"You're that too," Tyler replied. He gently pulled up the covers over Kelsey's naked body.

"I'm OK."

"I don't want you to get cold," Tyler replied.

Kelsey snuggled against him. "You're so good to me," she said happily.

"The feeling is mutual."

"I just want to lie here forever."

"I wish we could," Tyler replied.

"We can stay for a while."

"Not too long. Athena, what time is it?"

"The time is 3:30."

"We have a half hour." Tyler said, holding her close.

"We have a half hour until what?"

Tyler sighed. "Zach's coming back over."

"Why?"

"He wants to go ring-shopping with you."

"Today?"

"He's going to talk to his parents about Reina tomorrow, and he wants to know how much the ring's going to cost, so he can talk his parents into paying for it."

"And you agreed to this?"

"Zach said if we went today, I wouldn't hear about his relationship with Reina for at least two weeks. It seemed like a good deal."

Kelsey giggled.

"You and Zach have the strangest friendship," she commented.

An hour later, Kelsey, Tyler, and Zachary were standing inside a jewelry store in the luxury mall that was a couple of miles from Lisa's house.

"I want something a little bigger than that one," Zach was saying to the clerk.

"How about this one?" the clerk asked, pulling out a glittering diamond ring.

"What do you think, Kels?" Zach asked her.

Kelsey looked at the ring closely. Because of Tyler's many gifts of jewelry to her, Kelsey was developing an eye for quality.

"It's pretty," she said noncommittally.

"Remember, I can't afford the kind of diamonds you wear, Mrs. Olsen," Zach said. The clerk smiled at the joke. Everyone in the store had recognized the Olsen couple the second that they had walked in, but as Kelsey knew, being in the Olsen family was only newsworthy outside the Pacific Northwest. She felt a comfort here than she hadn't felt in New York, and it wasn't just because she and Tyler could travel without security. The Olsens were just one of the many tech billionaire families in the region, and although they were treated with respect, they weren't fawned over.

"I think that Reina would appreciate a more classic style," Kelsey said. "Can we see that one?" she asked the clerk.

"Of course," the clerk said, pulling the ring out for them. She set it down on the black velvet tray in front of Zach, and Kelsey picked it up. She looked at it carefully.

"This one," she said firmly, setting it back on the tray.

"Mrs. Olsen has spoken," Zach said. He took out his phone and snapped a photo of the sparkling ring. It was beautiful, a little smaller than Kelsey's, with a pear-shaped cut.

"How much?" he asked the clerk.

Instead of speaking, the clerk picked up a calculator and typed in the price. Then she showed the calculator to Zach.

Tyler looked over Zach's shoulder at the price.

"Mrs. Olsen has expensive taste," Zach commented. He looked at Tyler. "This is your fault." Zach said to him. "Kelsey North would have picked something cheaper."

"You don't have to get engaged," Tyler pointed out.

"Yes, I do," Zach said, making a note of the price in his phone. "Thank you," he said to the clerk. "Thank you, too, Kelsey, I think."

"You can eat ramen for a few weeks to pay for it," Kelsey said as they headed out of the store.

"A few years? I guess so," Zach commented.

"You're going to talk your parents into paying for it anyway," Tyler said, putting his arm around Kelsey's waist.

"Considering the measly salary they pay me, it's the least that they can do," Zach replied.

"When are you going to talk to them?"

"This weekend. Then everyone will have six weeks to talk me out of this."

"Your parents are going to think this is a great idea, and I'm done discussing it with you," Tyler said. "Kelsey and I are going to spend a relaxing weekend in Vancouver with the Perkins family, and we're going to move on with our lives."

"Then I'll be asking Reina to marry me on Valentine's Day. Mark your calendars," Zach said brightly.

"I won't, but OK," Tyler said.

"Kelsey's rooting for me. She knows how special Reina is," Zach commented.

"I do," Kelsey said, but like Tyler, she had her concerns. She just hadn't expressed them to Zach.

"Well, I'm off. I need to pick up my new suit," Zach said. He gave Kelsey a hug. "Thanks for your help, Kels."

"Any time," Kelsey said.

"Bye," Zach said, and he wandered off.

"So what do you want to do? Hang around here? Head back?" Tyler asked.

"Let's walk," Kelsey said. Now that it was after Christmas, the mall was quiet.

"OK," Tyler said, caressing her hand with his own. They began to walk slowly, luxury stores on either side of them.

"Are you looking forward to Vancouver tomorrow?" Tyler asked her.

"Very much," Kelsey said, but as she spoke, she remembered Jessica, and Jessica's words to her.

"Tyler," Kelsey said.

"Yes?"

"Tell me about Quinn."

Want my unreleased 5000-word story
Introducing the Billionaire Boys Club
and other free gifts from time to time?

Then join my mailing list at

http://www.caramillerbooks.com/inner-circle/

Subscribe now and read it now!

You can also follow me on Twitter and Facebook